Scholastic Success With

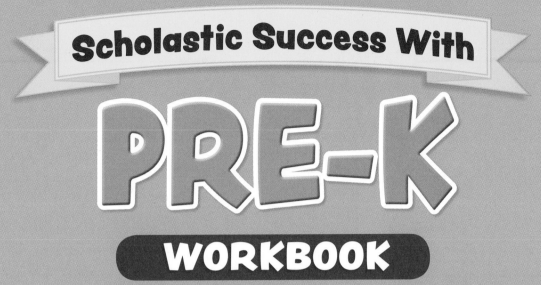

PRE-K

WORKBOOK

■SCHOLASTIC

NEW YORK • TORONTO • LONDON • AUCKLAND • SYDNEY
MEXICO CITY • NEW DELHI • HONG KONG • BUENOS AIRES

Pages 321–346 taken or adapted from *First Homework: Alphabet* by Alyse Sweeney © 2010 Alyse Sweeney.

Other pages were previously published in: *Now I Know My Alphabet; Now I Know My Numbers;* and *Now I Know My Colors, Shapes & Patterns.*

Cover and interior design by Michelle H. Kim
Interior illustrations by Maxie Chambliss, Rusty Fletcher, Lucia Kemp Henry, and Rob McClurkan

ISBN 978-1-338-06022-5

Table of Contents

ALPHABET

COUNTING AND PATTERNS

PHONICS

© Scholastic Inc.

MY FIRST ALPHABET BOOKS

© Scholastic Inc.

Dear Parent:

Congratulations on choosing this wonderful resource for your child. For nearly a century, Scholastic has been a leader in educational publishing, creating quality materials for use in schools and at home. At Scholastic, we firmly believe that it is never too early to begin the learning journey—especially when that journey includes a treasure trove of fun, skill-building activities that are just right for pre-K kids.

To help your child make the most of the learning opportunities in this "first" workbook, try these helpful hints:

★ Choose a cozy place to work that is free of distractions. Make sure you have pencils and crayons on hand.

★ Enjoy frequent learning sessions, but keep them short. Ten to 15 minutes is an ideal length of time for most young learners.

★ Work together to cut out, staple, and complete the 26 *My First Alphabet Books* on pages 365 to 416. Sharing these little books with your child will help jumpstart their reading ability.

★ Praise your child's successes and encourage his or her efforts. The stickers on page 417 are a great way to say, "Job well done!"

★ Offer positive support when your child needs extra help. If he or she begins to grow frustrated, take a break and revisit the topic at a later time.

On the pages that follow, you'll find hundreds of playful activities designed to keep your child engaged and challenged, but not overwhelmed. It is divided into six sections: Alphabet, Numbers, Colors and Shapes, Counting and Patterns, Phonics, and My First Alphabet Books. Although this workbook is structured to move your child along a learning continuum, feel free to use the pages in any order you choose. The Table of Contents includes a complete list of each activity along with the skill it addresses.

Take the lead and help your child master essential early skills with the *Scholastic Success With Pre-K Workbook*. (Turn the page to see a complete list of focus skills.) The time is right to start your child on the path to a lifetime of learning success!

FOCUS SKILLS

The playful activities in this workbook reinforce age-appropriate skills to help your young learner meet—and exceed—the rigorous standards in school.

Alphabet

* ★ Identifying uppercase letters
* ★ Identifying lowercase letters
* ★ Writing uppercase letters
* ★ Writing lowercase letters
* ★ Sequencing letters
* ★ Understanding initial letter sounds

Numbers

* ★ Identifying numerals 1 to 10
* ★ Identifying number names *one* to *ten*
* ★ Writing numerals 1 to 10
* ★ Writing number names *one* to *ten*
* ★ Counting simple quantities
* ★ Drawing/representing simple quantities

Colors and Shapes

* ★ Identifying key colors
* ★ Identifying key shapes
* ★ Writing shape names
* ★ Writing color names
* ★ Drawing in colors
* ★ Creating shapes

Counting and Patterns

* ★ Counting to 10
* ★ Comparing sets
* ★ Understanding concept of fewer/more
* ★ Understanding concept of patterns
* ★ Completing simple color patterns
* ★ Completing simple shape patterns

Phonics

* ★ Understanding that print conveys meaning
* ★ Identifying and distinguishing initial letter sounds
* ★ Matching text to pictures

School Readiness

* ★ Building listening skills
* ★ Following directions
* ★ Performing steps in a sequence
* ★ Developing fine motor skills
* ★ Developing learning stamina

Creative Thinking

* ★ Exploring elements of own name
* ★ Drawing pictures from imagination
* ★ Completing open-ended sentence frames

ALPHABET

Circle each **A** on the **ANT**.

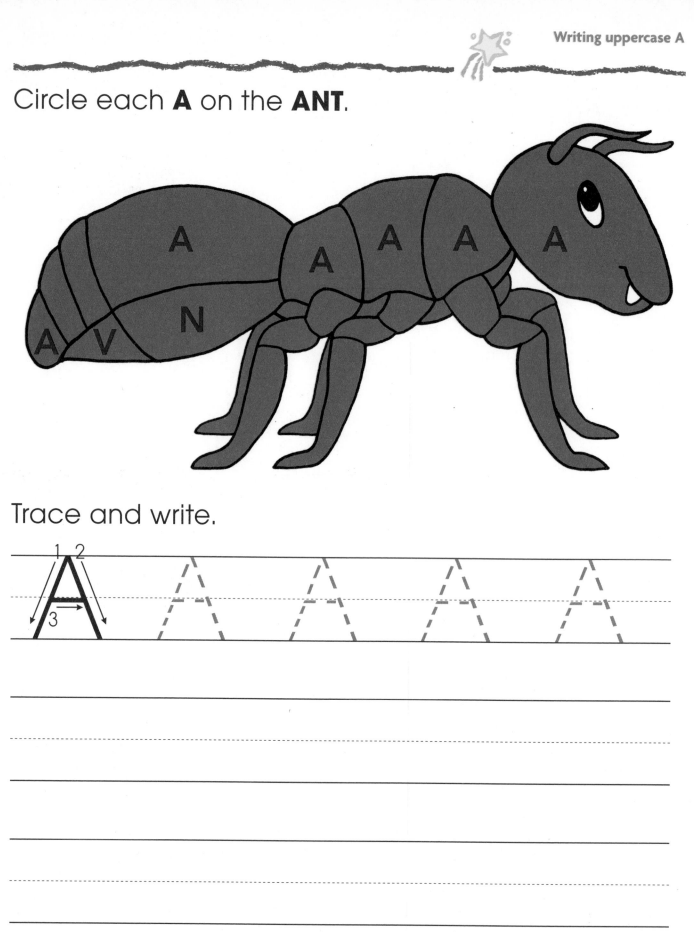

Trace and write.

Circle each item that begins with **A**.

Read the **a** words.

ant

apple

Trace and write.

Trace each apple shape. Write **a** on each one.

Find each **a**. Color that shape **red**.

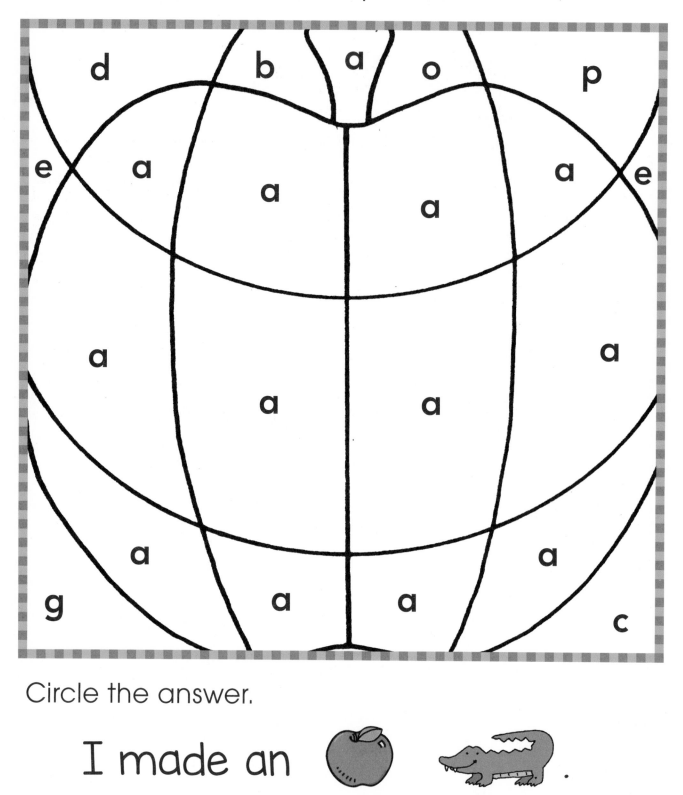

Circle the answer.

I made an

Write **A** to complete the word.

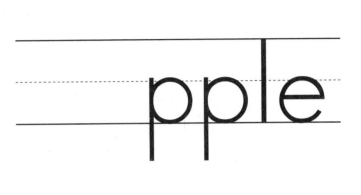

pple

Circle each **A**.

N	A	W
V	X	A
N	A	A

Circle each **a**.

c	a	e
d	c	a
a	b	a

Circle each **B** on the **BEAR**.

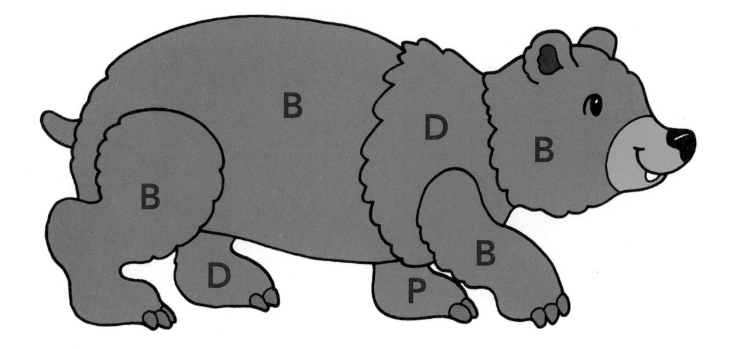

Trace and write.

Circle each item that begins with **B**.

Read the **b** words.

bear

balloon

Trace and write.

Trace each balloon. Write **b** on each one.

Find each **b**. Color that shape **blue**.

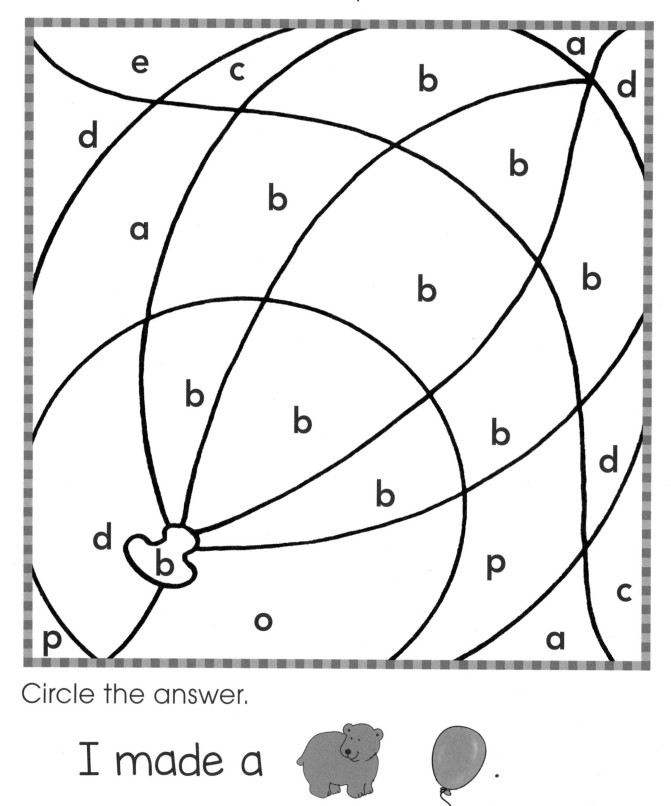

Circle the answer.

I made a

Write **B** to complete the word.

ear

Circle each **B**.

B	D	A
G	B	P
B	C	B

Circle each **b**.

b	a	b
d	c	b
b	e	a

Circle each **C** on the **CAT**.

Trace and write.

Circle each item that begins with **C**.

Read the **c** words.

cat

cupcake

Trace and write.

Trace each cupcake. Write **c** on each one.

Find each **c**. Color that shape **pink**.

Circle the answer.

I made a

Write **C** to complete the word.

at

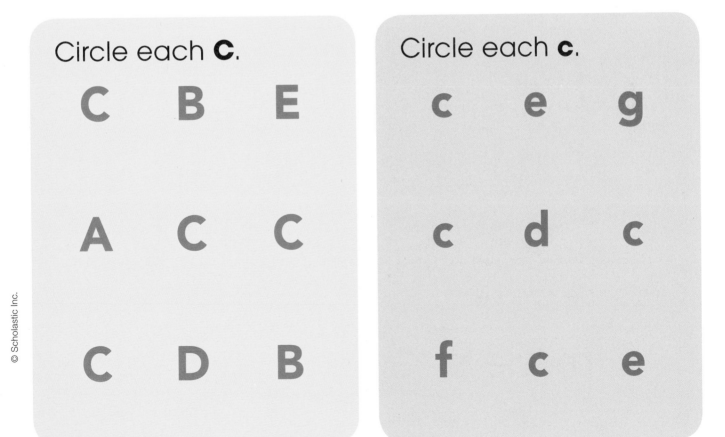

Circle each **C**.

C	B	E
A	C	C
C	D	B

Circle each **c**.

c	e	g
c	d	c
f	c	e

Circle each **D** on the **DOG**.

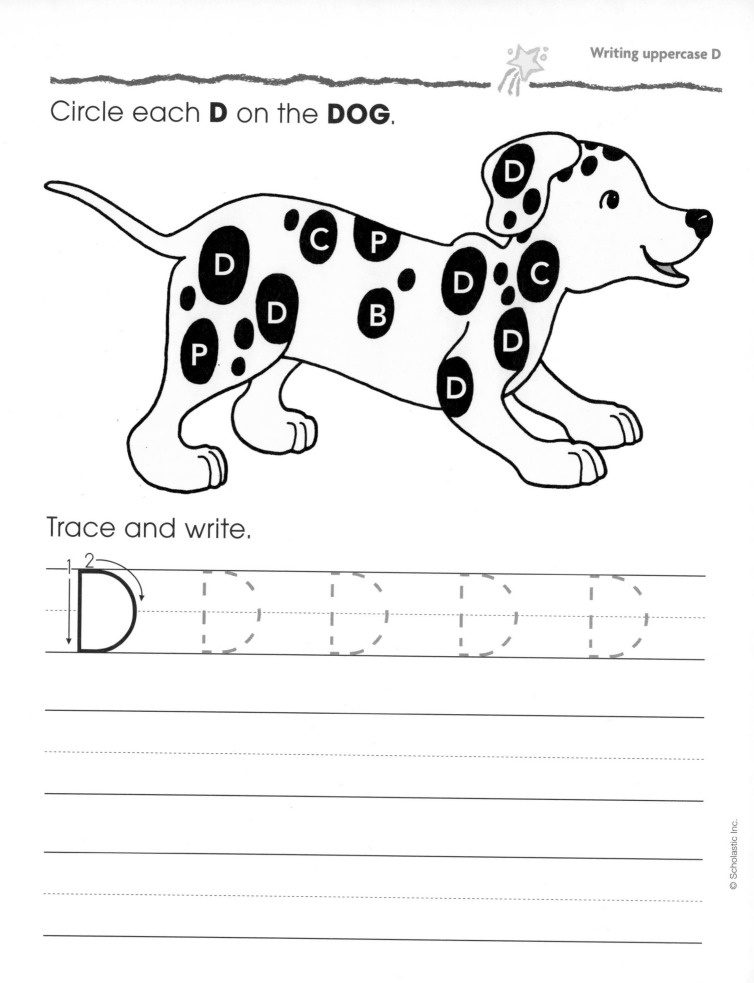

Trace and write.

Circle each item that begins with **D**.

Read the **d** words.

duck

dog

Trace and write.

Trace each duck. Write **d** on each one.

Find each **d**. Color that shape **yellow**.

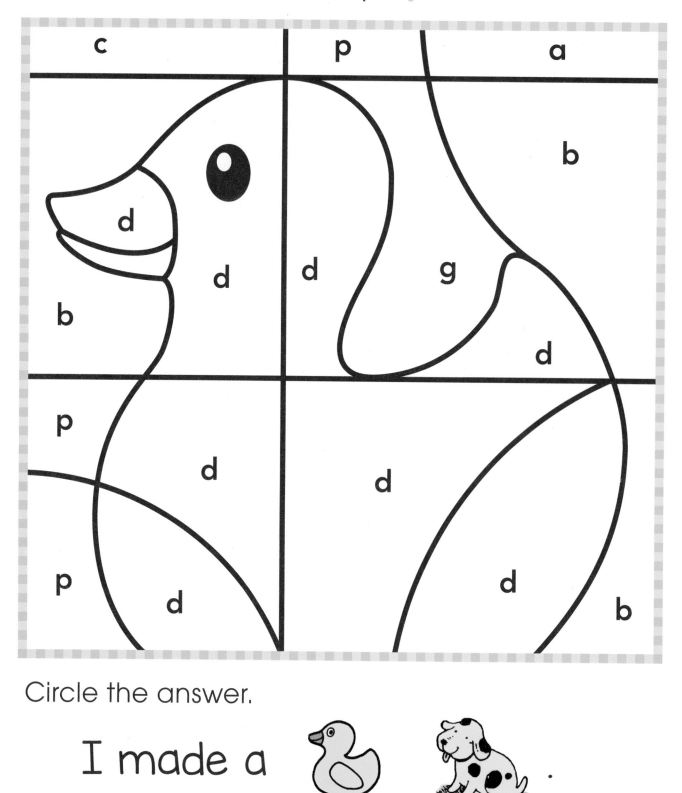

Circle the answer.

I made a   🦆   🐶   .

Write **D** to complete the word.

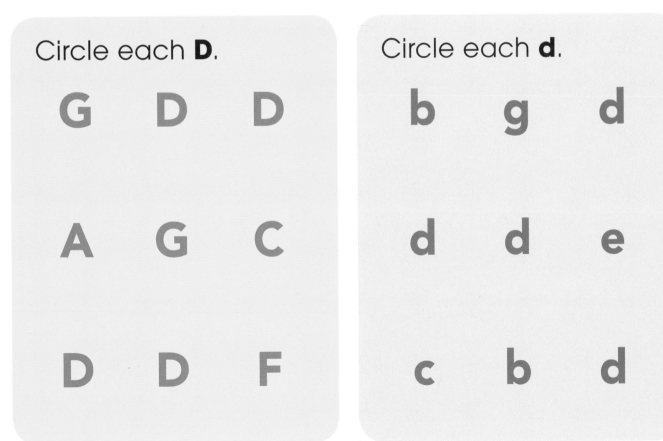

og

Circle each **D**.

G	D	D
A	G	C
D	D	F

Circle each **d**.

b	g	d
d	d	e
c	b	d

Circle each **E** on the **ELEPHANT**.

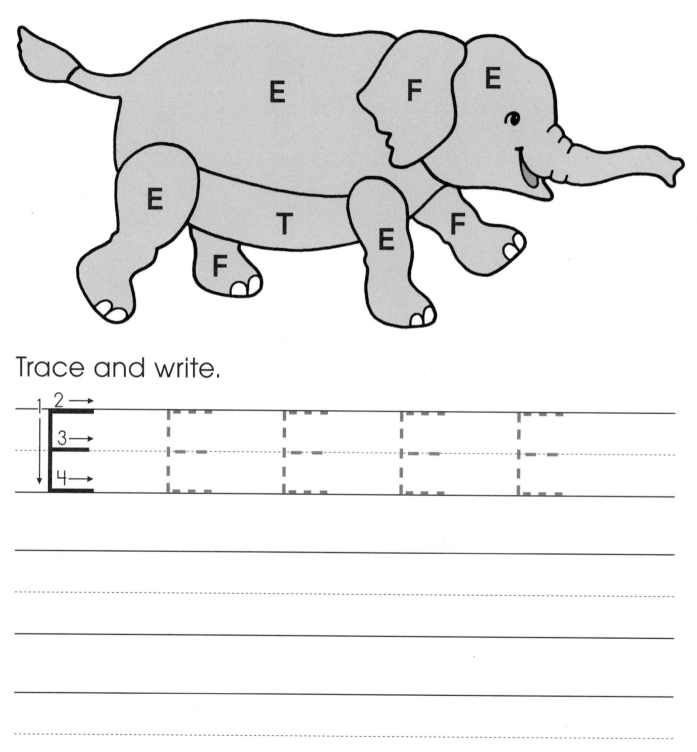

Trace and write.

Circle each item that begins with **E**.

Read the **e** words.

egg

elephant

Trace and write.

e

Trace each egg. Write **e** on each one.

Find each **e**. Color that shape **tan**.

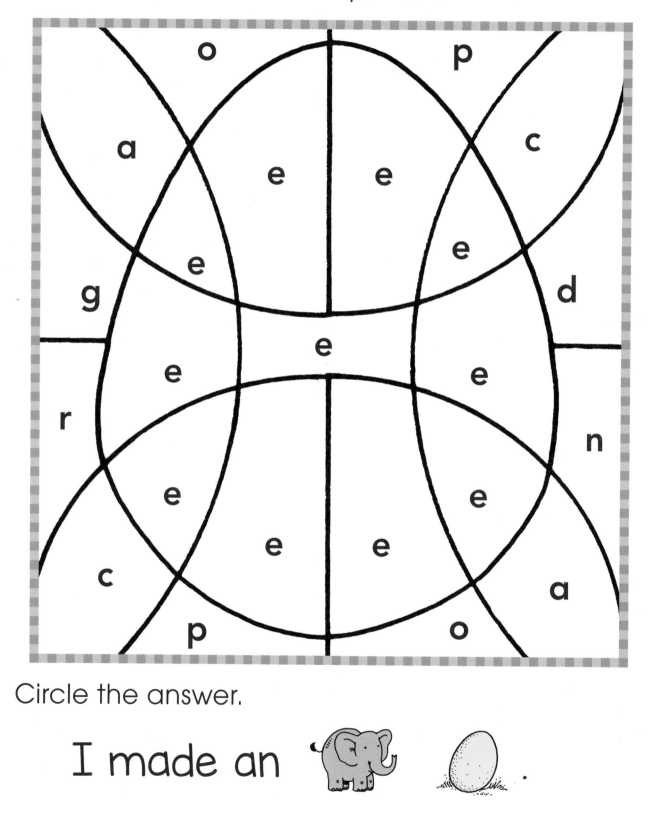

Circle the answer.

I made an

Write **E** to complete the word.

lephant

Circle each **E**.

E	E	D
P	G	D
E	G	E

Circle each **e**.

b	p	e
e	d	e
h	e	f

Circle each **F** on the **FOX**.

Trace and write.

Circle each item that begins with **F**.

Read the **f** words.

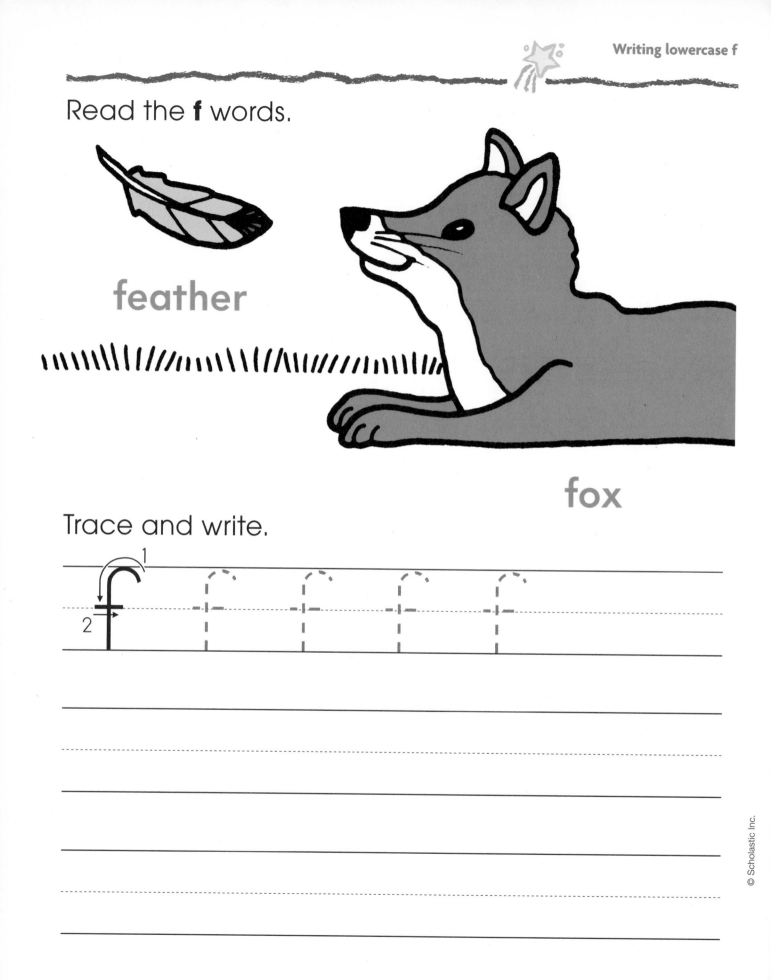

feather

fox

Trace and write.

Trace each feather. Write **f** on each one.

Find each **f**. Color that shape **blue**.

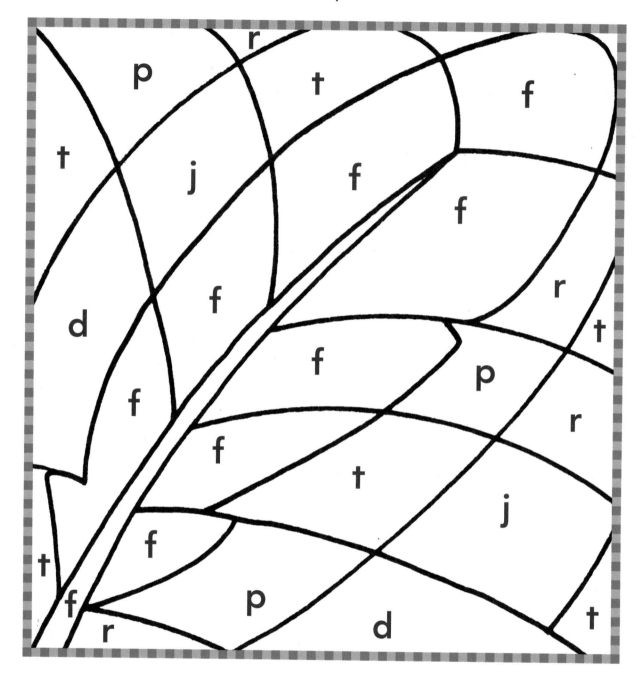

Circle the answer.

I made a  .

Write **F** to complete the word.

OX

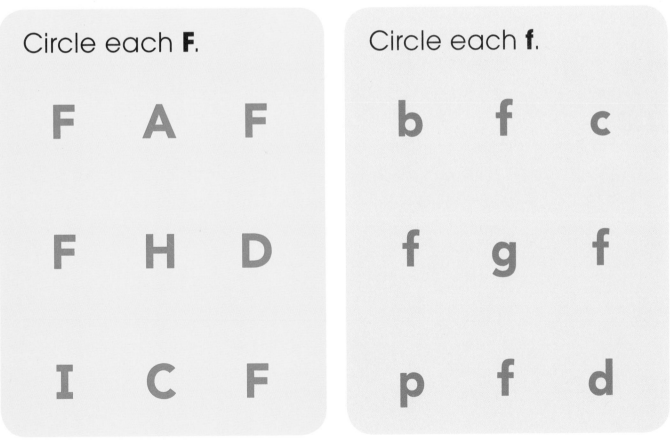

Circle each **F**.

F	A	F
F	H	D
I	C	F

Circle each **f**.

b	f	c
f	g	f
p	f	d

Circle each **G** in the **GARDEN**.

Trace and write.

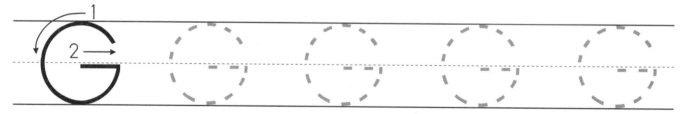

Circle each item that begins with **G**.

Read the **g** words.

gate

gopher

Trace and write.

Trace each gopher. Write **g** on each one.

Find each **g**. Color that shape **red**.

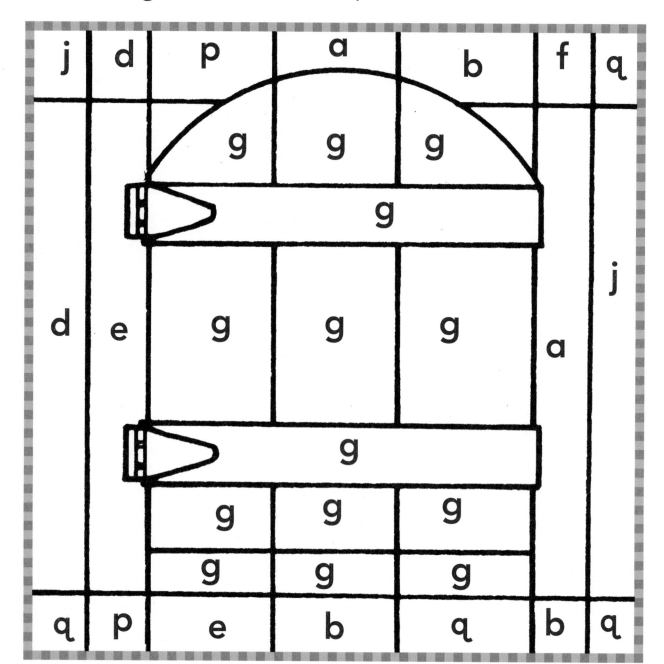

Circle the answer.

I made a

Write **G** to complete the word.

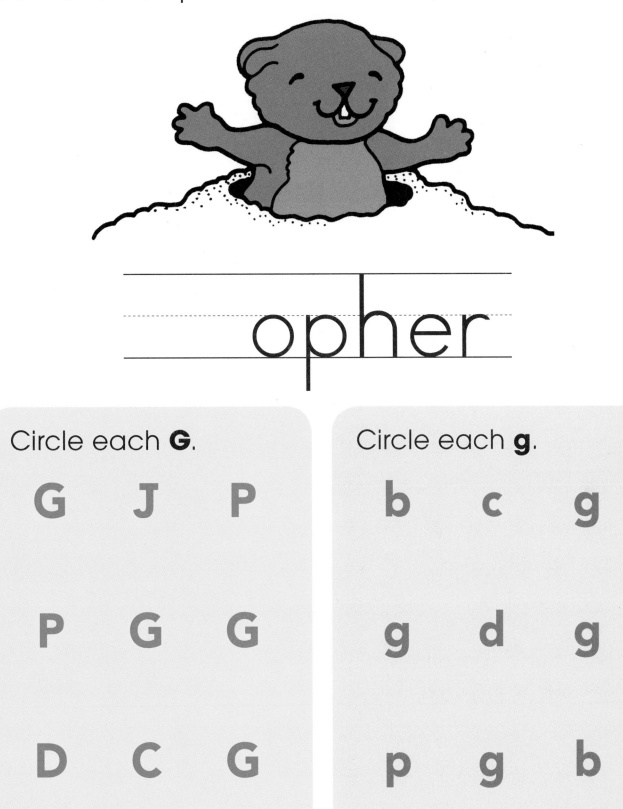

opher

Circle each **G**.

G	J	P
P	G	G
D	C	G

Circle each **g**.

b	c	g
g	d	g
p	g	b

Circle each **H** on the **HAMSTER** home.

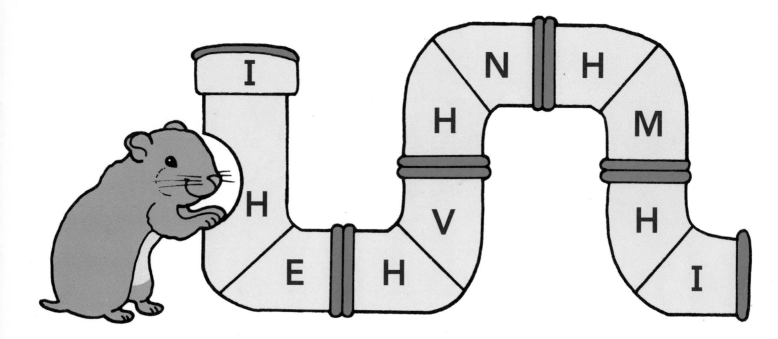

Trace and write.

Circle each item that begins with **H**.

Read the **h** words.

hat

hamster

Trace and write.

Trace each hat. Write **h** on each one.

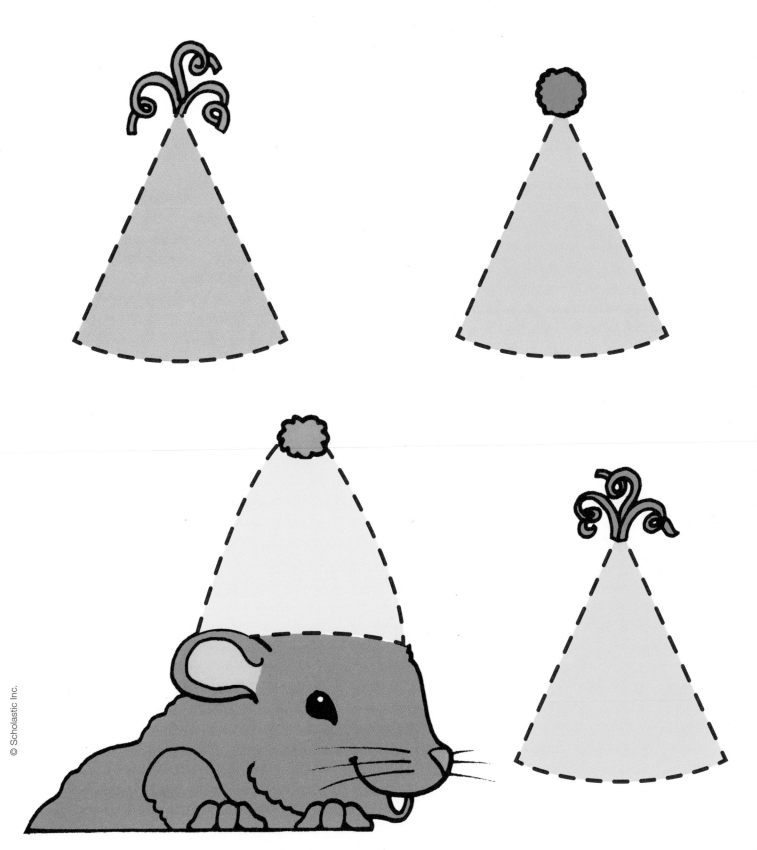

Find each **h**. Color that shape **pink**.

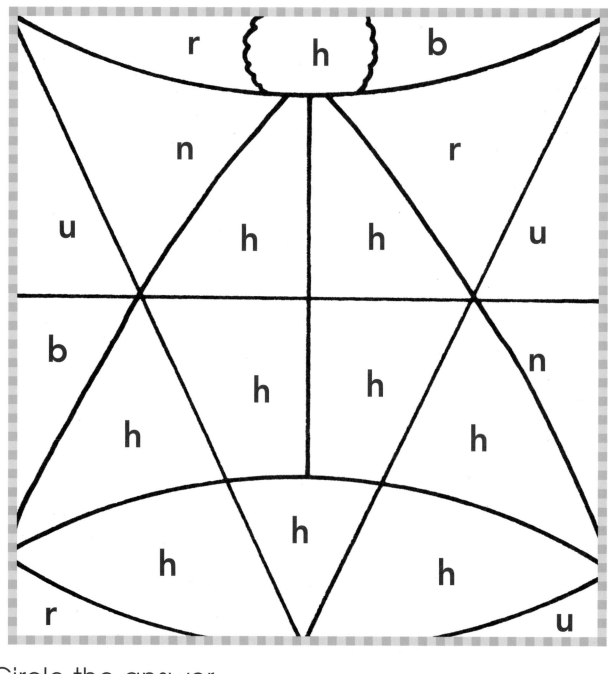

Circle the answer.

I made a   .

Write **H** to complete the word.

amster

Circle each **H**.

H	D	H
P	H	D
H	C	G

Circle each **h**.

b	p	h
h	a	h
e	h	f

Circle each **I** on the **IGUANA**.

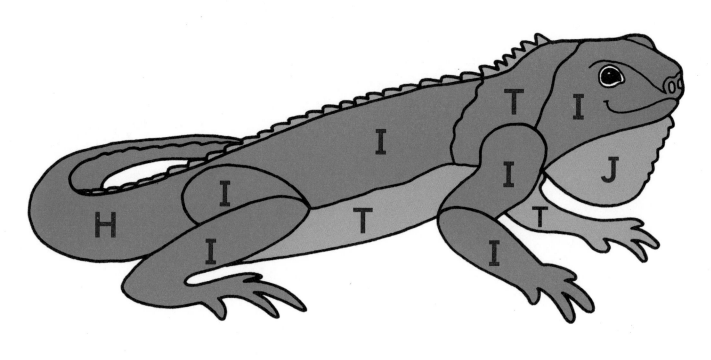

Trace and write.

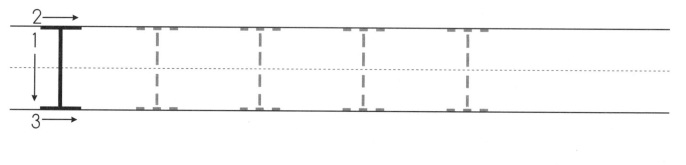

Circle each item that begins with **I**.

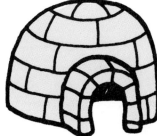

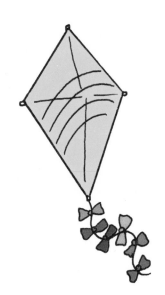

Read the **i** words.

insects

iguana

Trace and write.

2•

1↓

Trace each insect. Write **i** on each one.

Find each **i**. Color that shape **green**.

Circle the answer.

I made an

Write **I** to complete the word.

guana

Circle each **I**.

H	I	M
I	I	D
P	C	I

Circle each **i**.

b	p	c
h	i	i
i	i	h

Circle each **J** on the **JELLYFISH**.

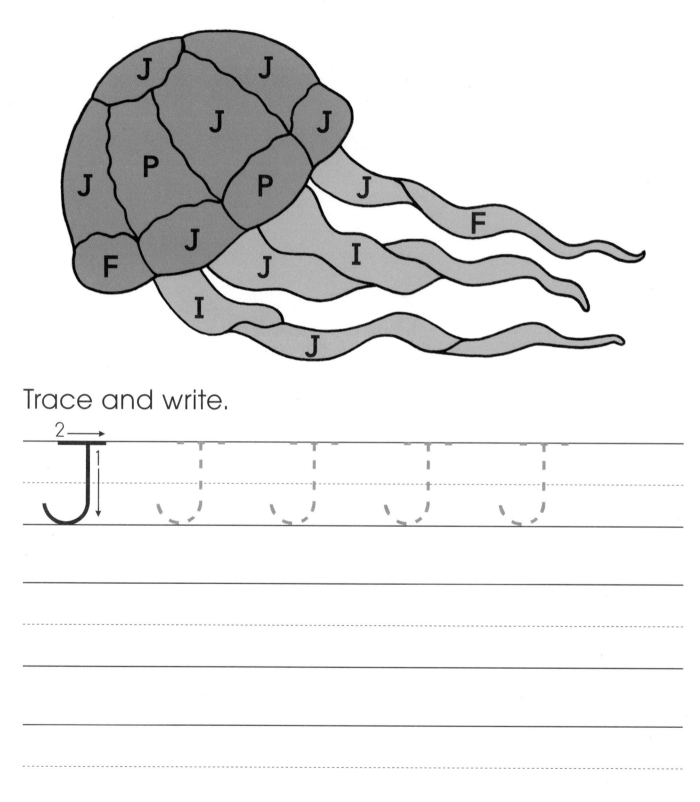

Trace and write.

Circle each item that begins with **J**.

Read the **j** words.

jellyfish

jacket

Trace and write.

Trace each jellyfish. Write **j** on each one.

Find each **j**. Color that shape **purple**.

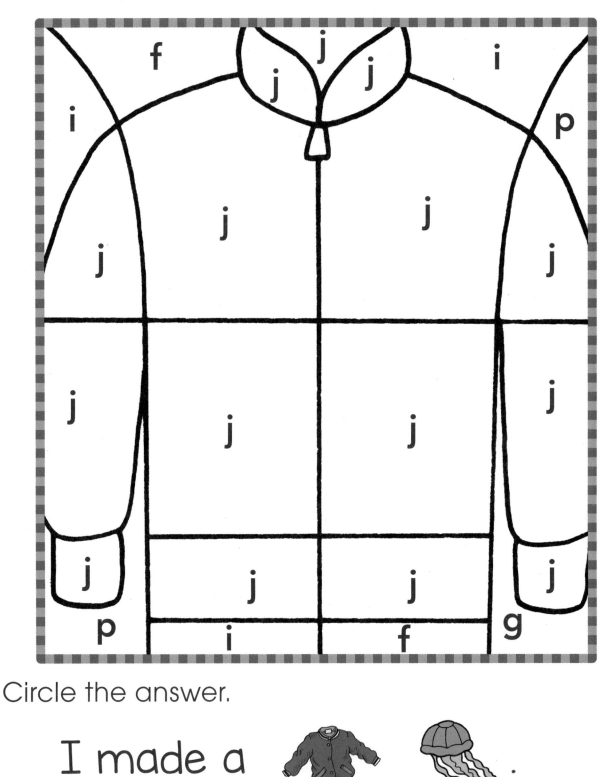

Circle the answer.

I made a   .

Write **J** to complete the word.

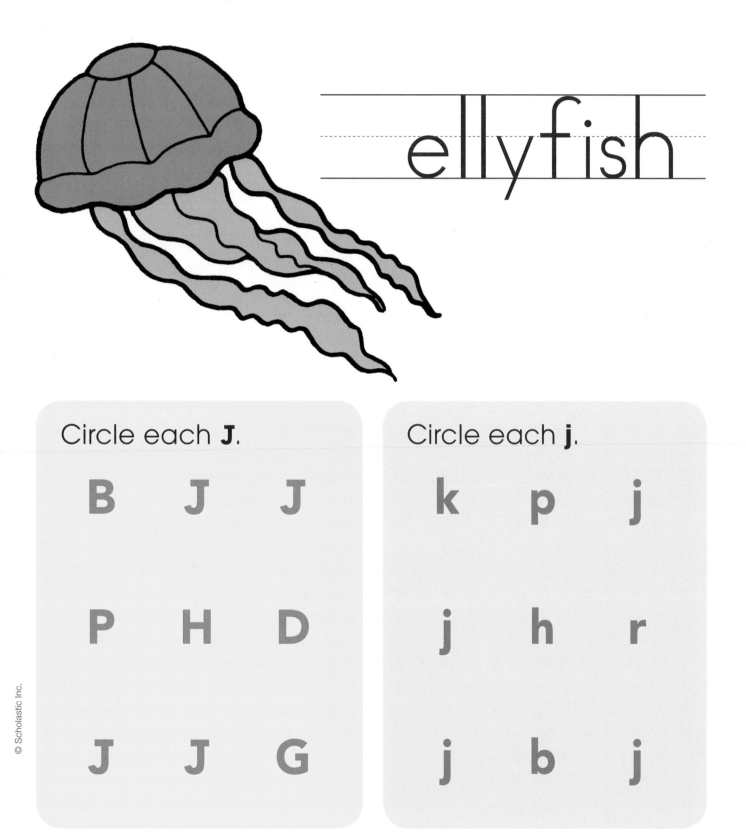

ellyfish

Circle each **J**.

B	J	J
P	H	D
J	J	G

Circle each **j**.

k	p	j
j	h	r
j	b	j

Circle each **K** on the **KANGAROO** and in the garden.

Trace and write.

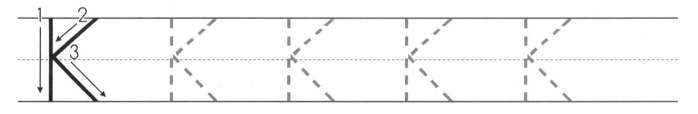

Circle each item that begins with **K**.

Read the **k** words.

kite

kangaroo

Trace and write.

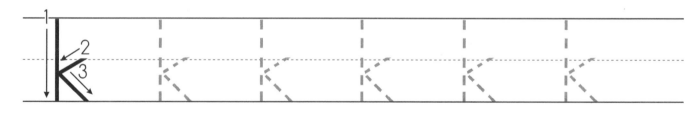

Trace each kite. Write **k** on each one.

Find each **k**. Color that shape **green**.

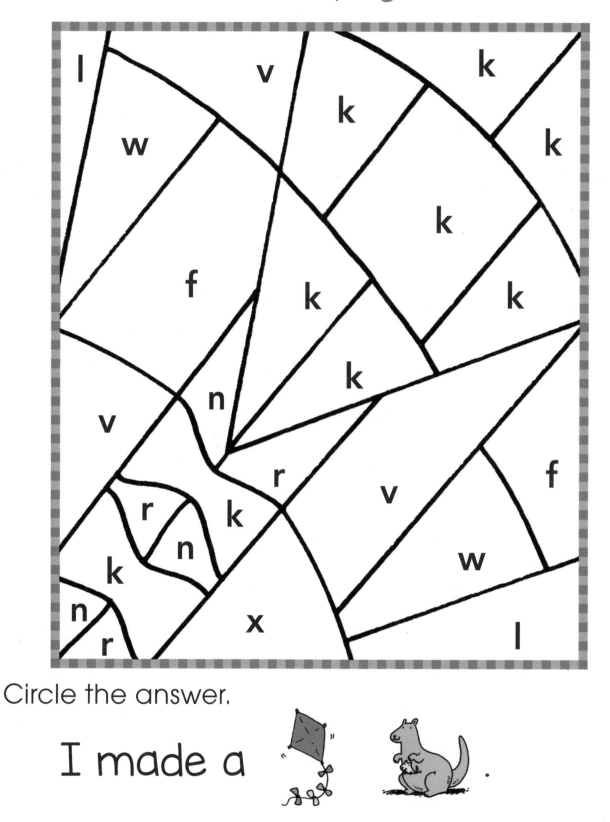

Circle the answer.

I made a

Write **K** to complete the word.

angaroo

Circle each **K**.	Circle each **k**.

K	**J**	**K**
P	**K**	**S**
J	**K**	**G**

k	**p**	**i**
k	**k**	**k**
j	**b**	**f**

© Scholastic Inc.

Circle each **L** on the **LION**.

Trace and write.

Circle each item that begins with **L**.

Read the **l** words.

lollipop

lion

Trace and write.

Trace each lollipop. Write **l** on each one.

Find each **l**. Color that shape **red**.

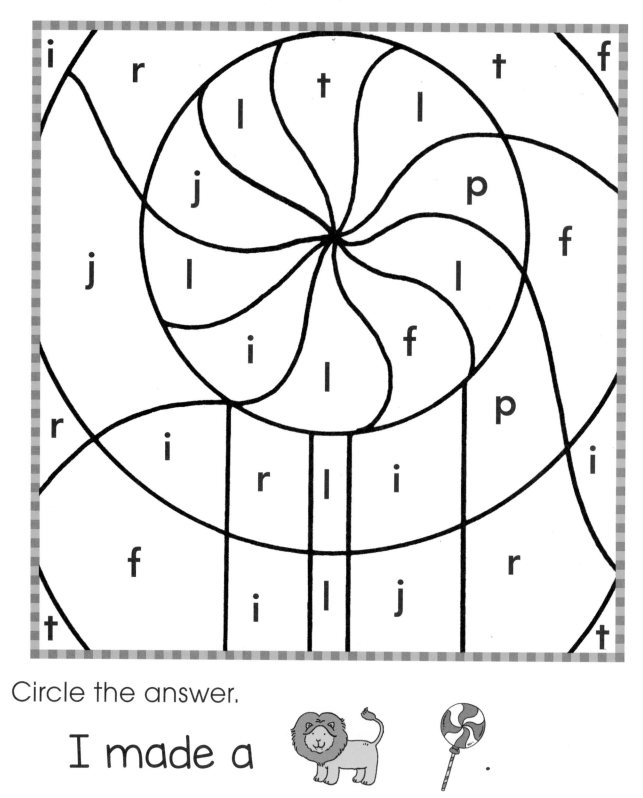

Circle the answer.

I made a ☐ ☐ .

Write **L** to complete the word.

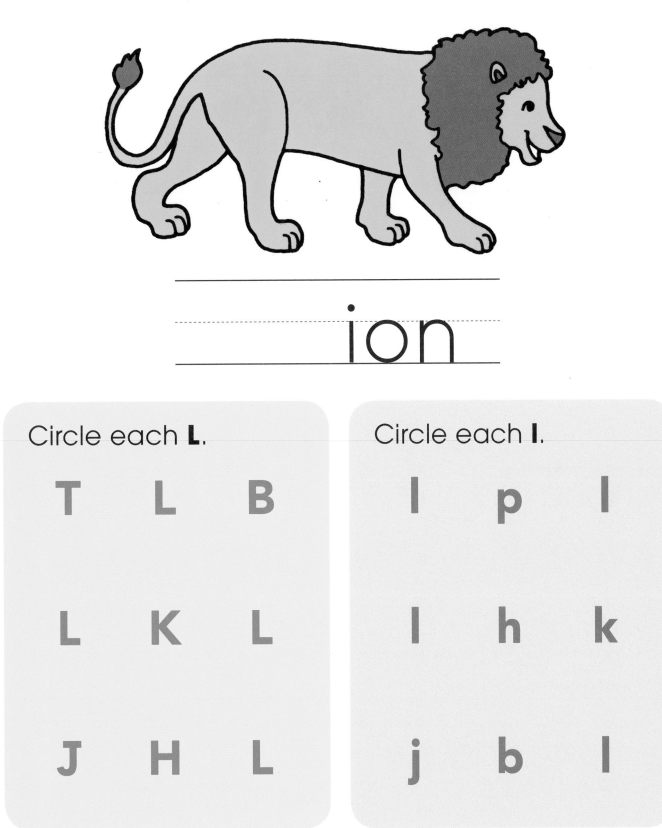

___ion

Circle each **L**.

T	L	B
L	K	L
J	H	L

Circle each **l**.

l	p	l
l	h	k
j	b	l

Circle each **M** on the **MITTENS**.

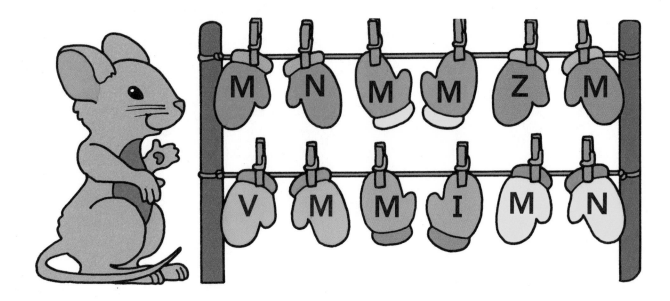

Trace and write.

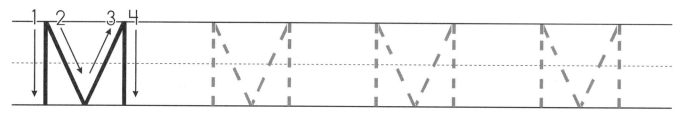

Circle each item that begins with **M**.

Read the **m** words.

mouse

mittens

Trace and write.

Trace each mitten. Write **m** on each one.

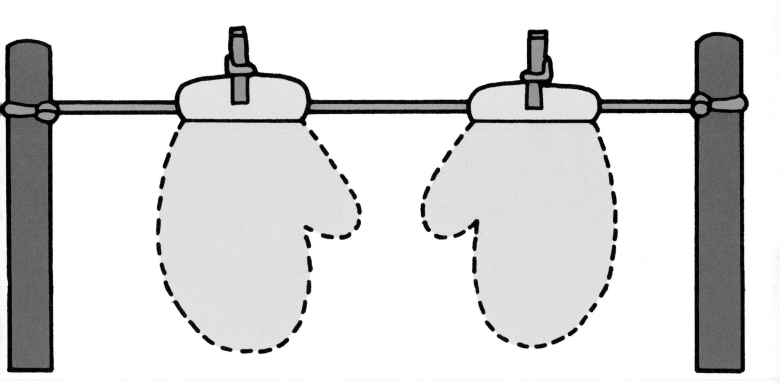

Find each **m**. Color that shape **blue**.

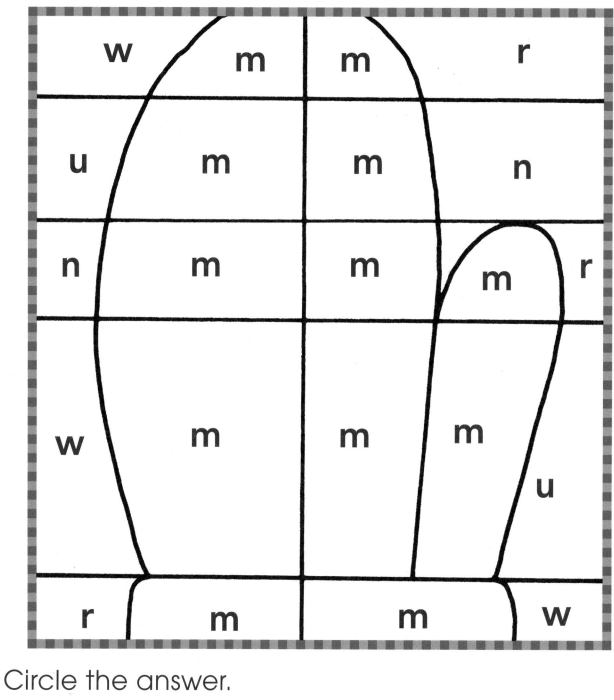

w	m	m	r
u	m	m	n
n	m	m	m r
w	m	m	m u
r	m	m	w

Circle the answer.

I made a  .

Write **M** to complete the word.

_____ouse

Circle each **M**.

M	P	U
J	M	D
M	G	M

Circle each **m**.

m	p	s
h	q	m
j	m	m

Circle each **N** on the **NEWT** and the grass.

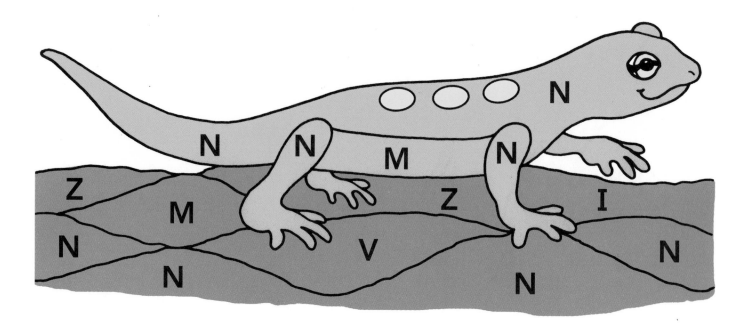

Trace and write.

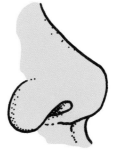

Circle each item that begins with **N**.

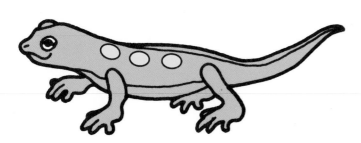

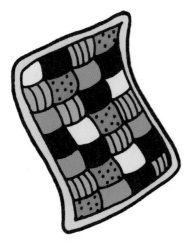

Read the **n** words.

newt

net

Trace and write.

n n n n n n n

Trace each net. Write **n** on each one.

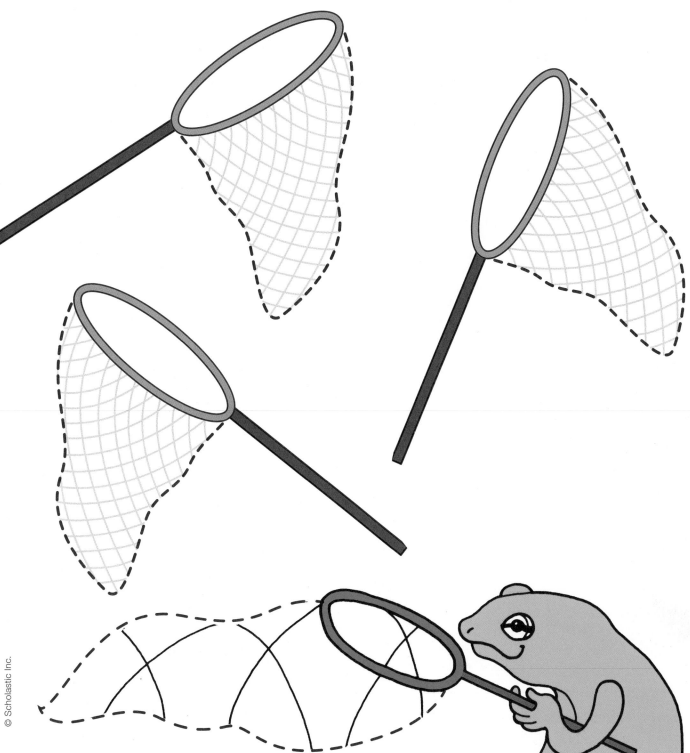

Find each **n**. Color that shape **orange**.

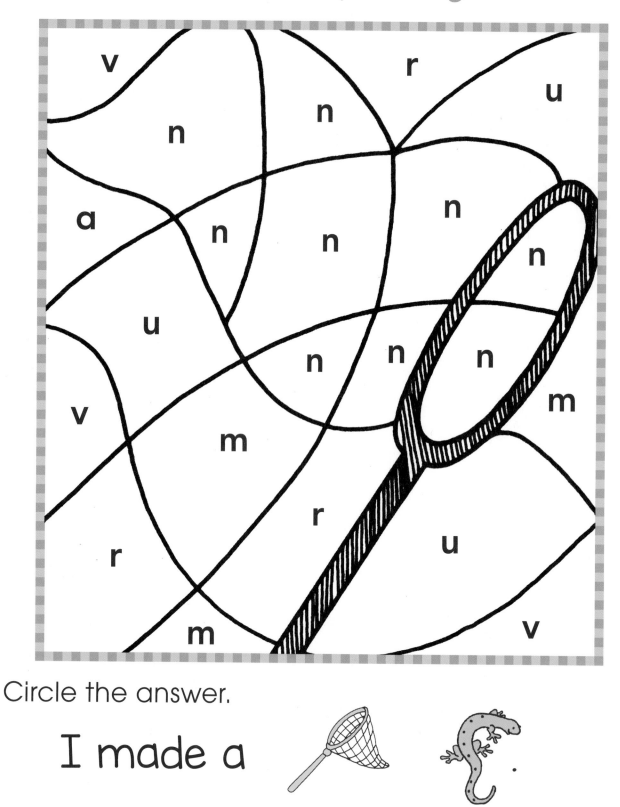

Circle the answer.

I made a

Write **N** to complete the word.

_____

_____ ewt

Circle each **N**.

N	J	P
N	G	R
U	N	N

Circle each **n**.

b	p	n
s	n	v
n	n	h

Circle each **O** on the **OTTER** and the bushes.

Trace and write.

Circle each item that begins with **O**.

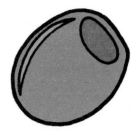

Read the **o** words.

otter

olive

Trace and write.

Trace each olive. Write o on each one.

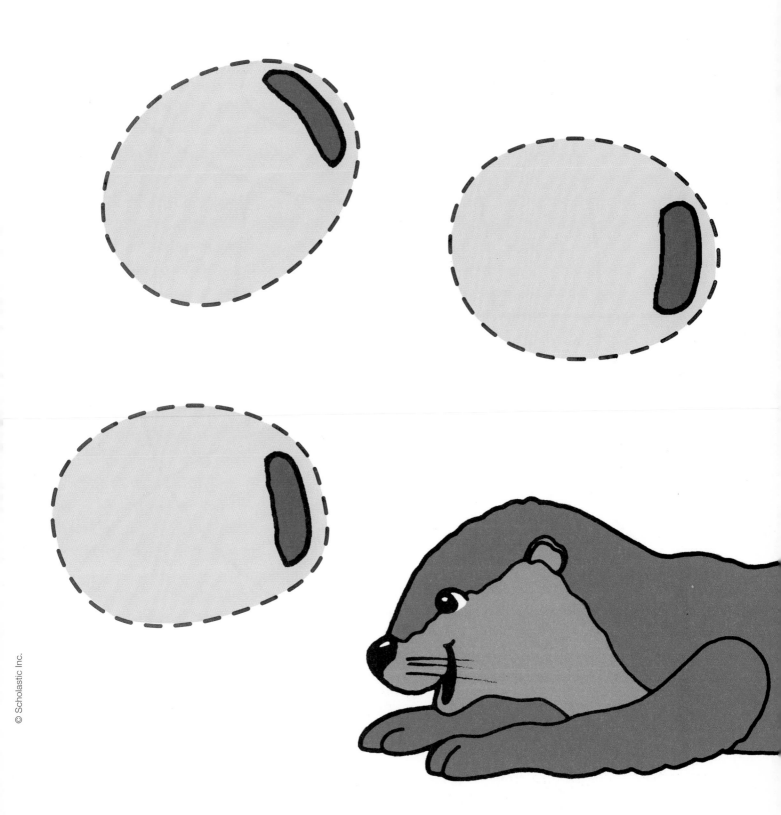

Find each **o**. Color that shape **green**.

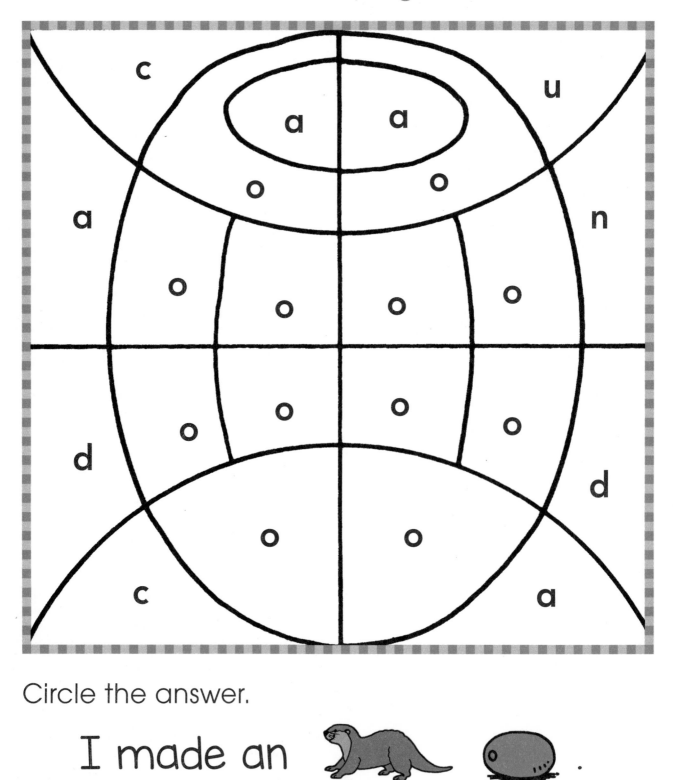

Circle the answer.

I made an

Write **O** to complete the word.

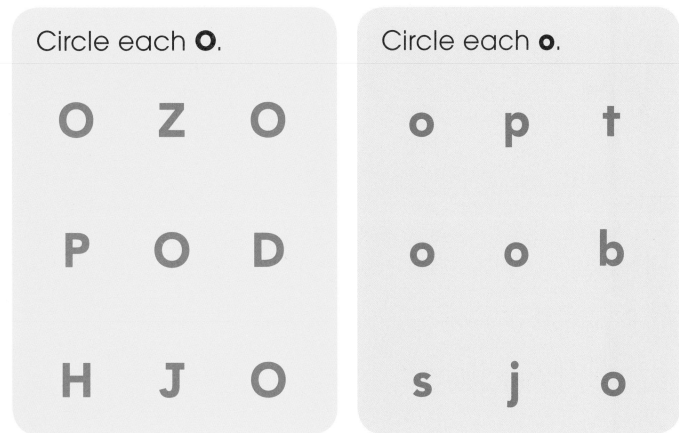

_____tter

Circle each **O**.

O	Z	O
P	O	D
H	J	O

Circle each **o**.

o	p	t
o	o	b
s	j	o

Circle each **P** on the **POODLE**.

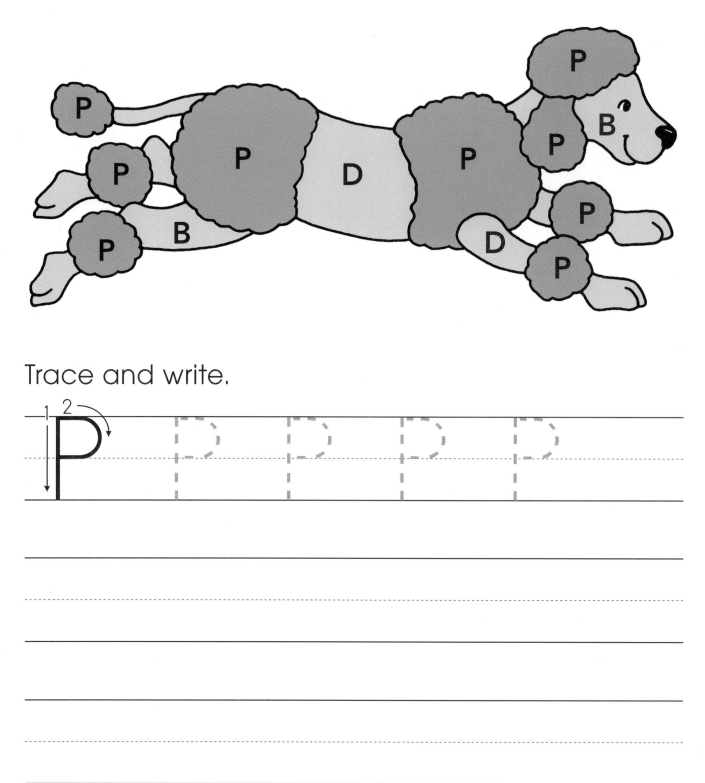

Trace and write.

Circle each item that begins with **P**.

Read the **p** words.

poodle   purse

Trace and write.

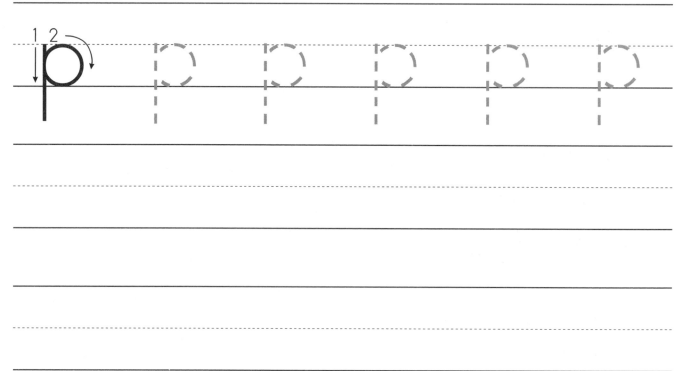

Trace each purse. Write **p** on each one.

Find each **p**. Color that shape **pink**.

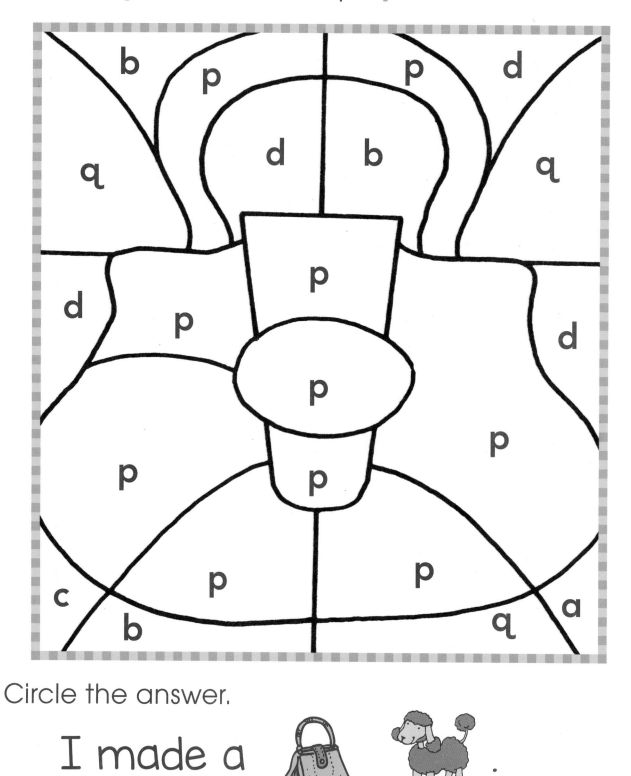

Circle the answer.

I made a 🛍️ 🐩 .

Write **P** to complete the word.

oodle

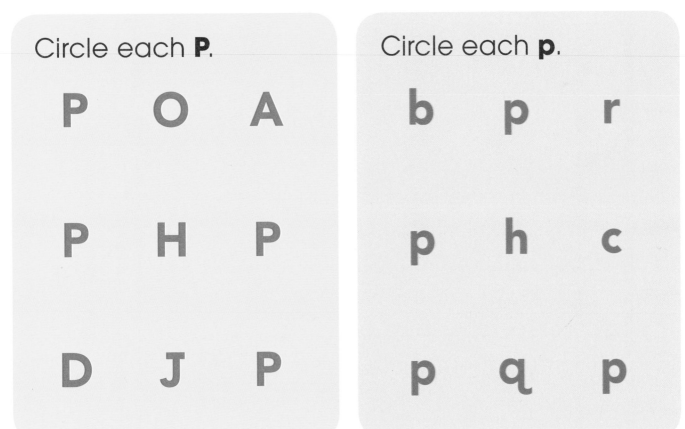

Circle each **P**.

P	O	A
P	H	P
D	J	P

Circle each **p**.

b	p	r
p	h	c
p	q	p

Circle each **Q** on the **QUAILS**.

Trace and write.

Circle each item that begins with **Q**.

Read the **q** words.

quilt

quail

Trace and write.

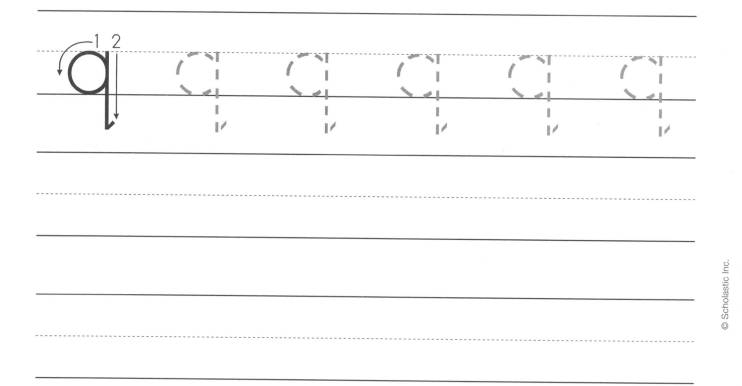

Trace each quilt square. Write **q** on each one.

Find each q. Color that shape **orange**.

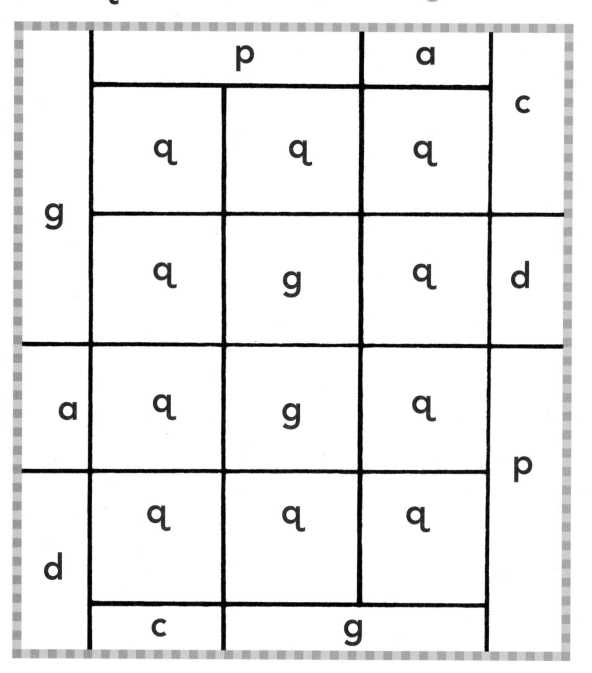

	p	a
	q	q	q	c
g	q	g	q	d
a	q	g	q	
d	q	q	q	p
	c	g	

Circle the answer.

I made a  .

Write **Q** to complete the word.

uail

Circle each **Q**.

M	Q	U
Q	Q	D
M	Q	M

Circle each **q**.

m	p	q
q	q	y
a	q	e

Circle each **R** on the **RACOON**.

Trace and write.

Circle each item that begins with **R**.

Read the **r** words.

radish

racoon

Trace and write.

Trace each radish. Write **r** on each one.

Find each **r**. Color that shape **red**.

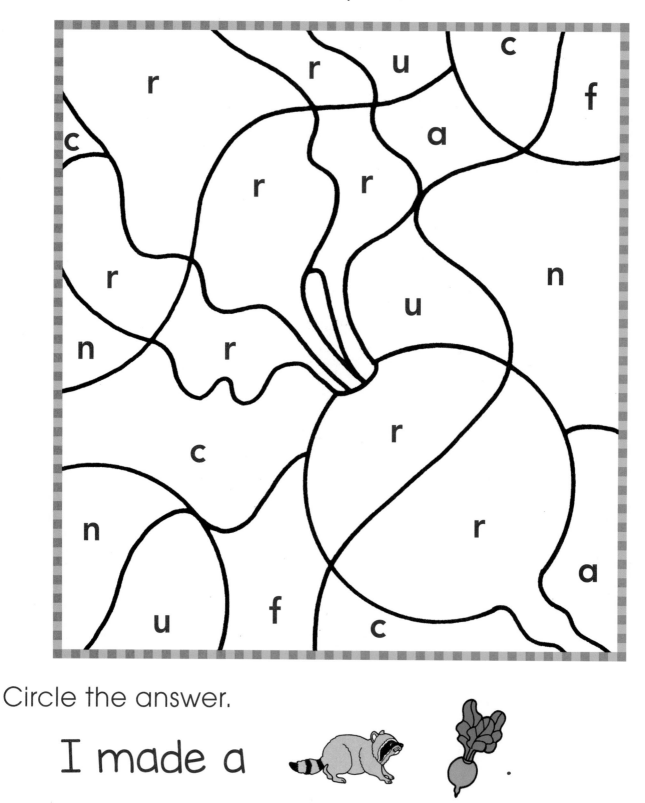

Circle the answer.

I made a

Write **R** to complete the word.

_____

accoon

_____

Circle each **R**.	Circle each **r**.
R P R	b r r
P R Q	v q r
R F J	m r p

Circle each **S** on the **SEAGULL**.

Trace and write.

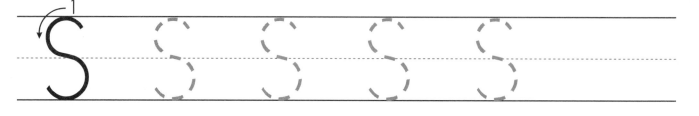

Circle each item that begins with **S**.

Read the **s** words.

seagull

soup

Trace and write.

Trace each soup cracker. Write **s** on each one.

Find each **s**. Color that shape **red**.

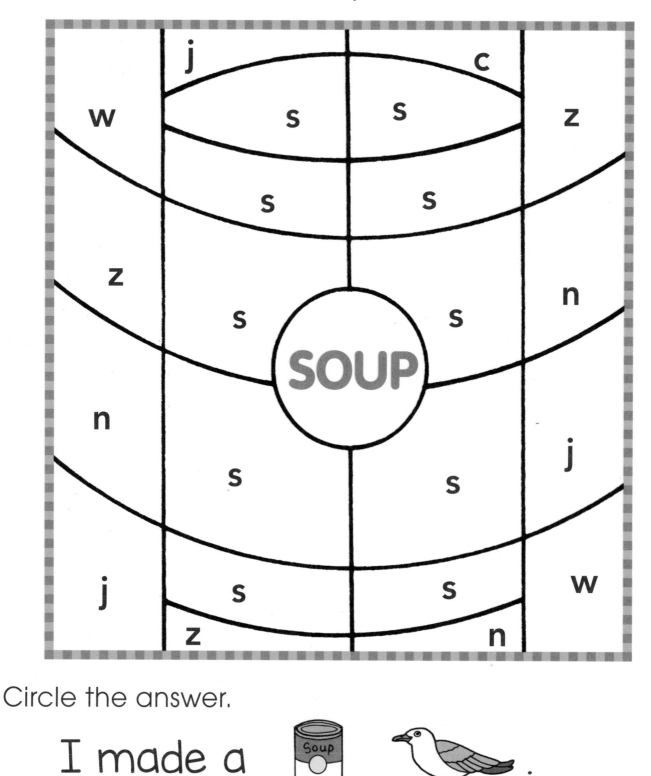

Circle the answer.

I made a

Write **S** to complete the word.

eagull

Circle each **S**.

S	J	S
O	S	P
F	S	N

Circle each **s**.

b	p	s
s	q	s
g	z	s

Circle each **T** on the **TURTLE**.

Trace and write.

Circle each item that begins with **T**.

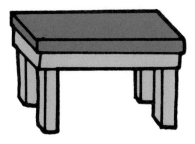

© Scholastic Inc.

Read the **t** words.

turtle

tent

Trace and write.

Trace each turtle. Write **t** on each one.

Find each **t**. Color that shape **green**.

Circle the answer.

I made a   .

Write **T** to complete the word.

_____urtle

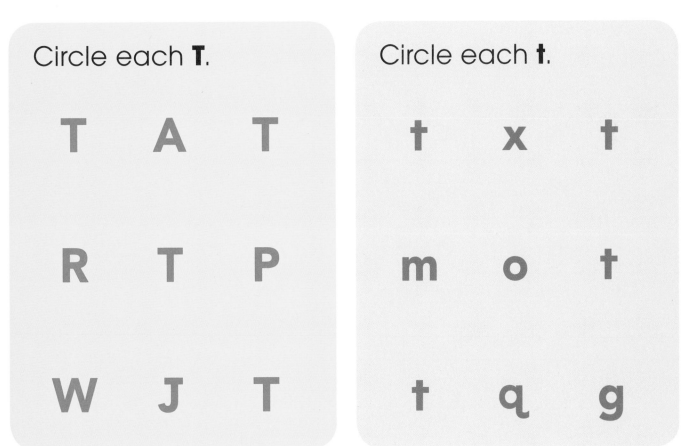

Circle each **T**.

T	A	T
R	T	P
W	J	T

Circle each **t**.

t	x	t
m	o	t
t	q	g

Circle each **U** on the **UNICORN**.

Trace and write.

Circle each item that begins with **U**.

Read the **u** words.

umbrella

unicorn

Trace and write.

Trace each umbrella. Write **u** on each one.

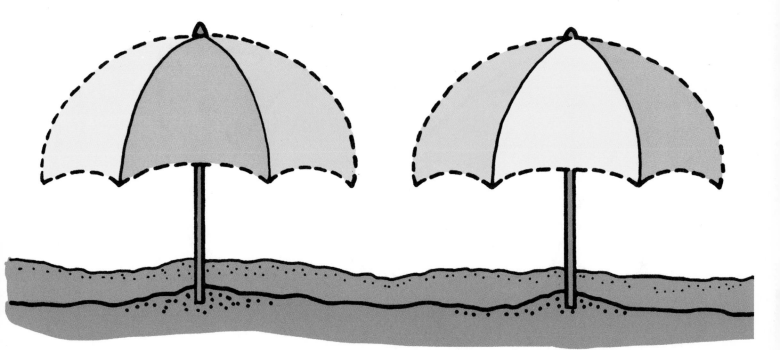

Find each **u**. Color that shape **purple**.

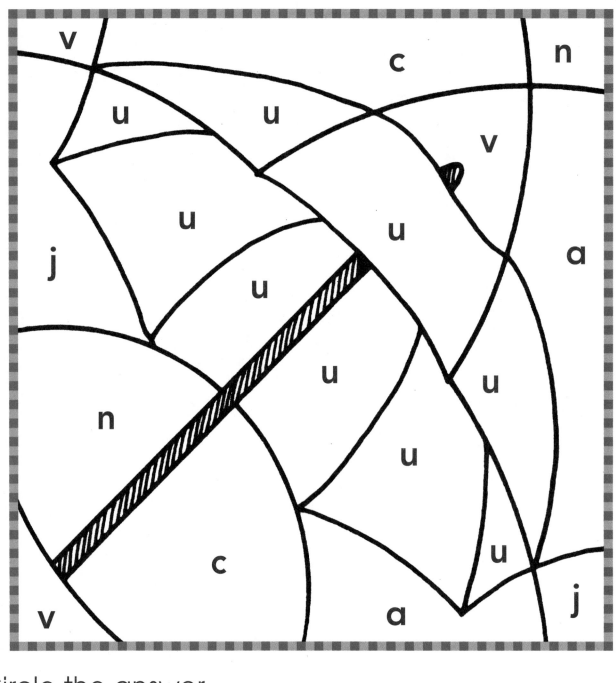

Circle the answer.

I made an   .

Write **U** to complete the word.

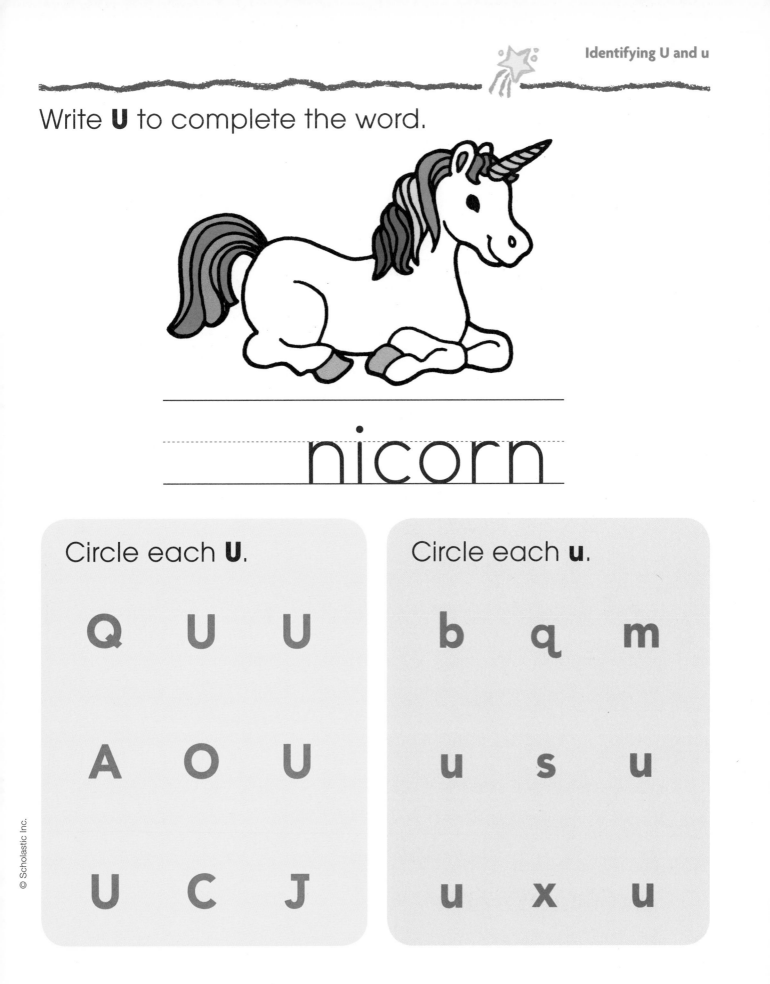

_____nicorn

Circle each **U**.

Q	U	U
A	O	U
U	C	J

Circle each **u**.

b	q	m
u	s	u
u	x	u

Circle each **V** on the **VULTURE**.

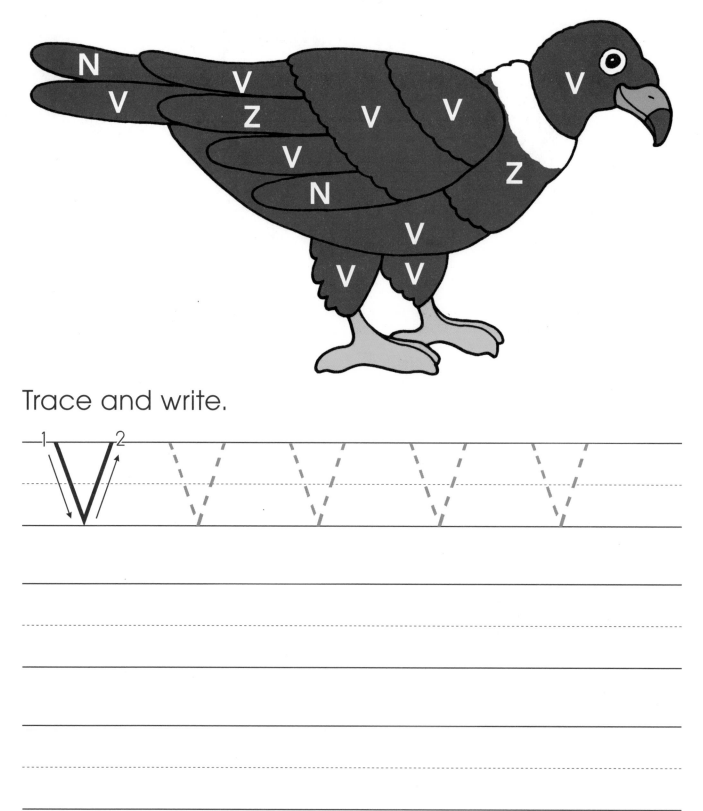

Trace and write.

Circle each item that begins with **V**.

Read the **v** words.

Trace and write.

Trace each van. Write **v** on each one.

Find each **v**. Color that shape **blue**.

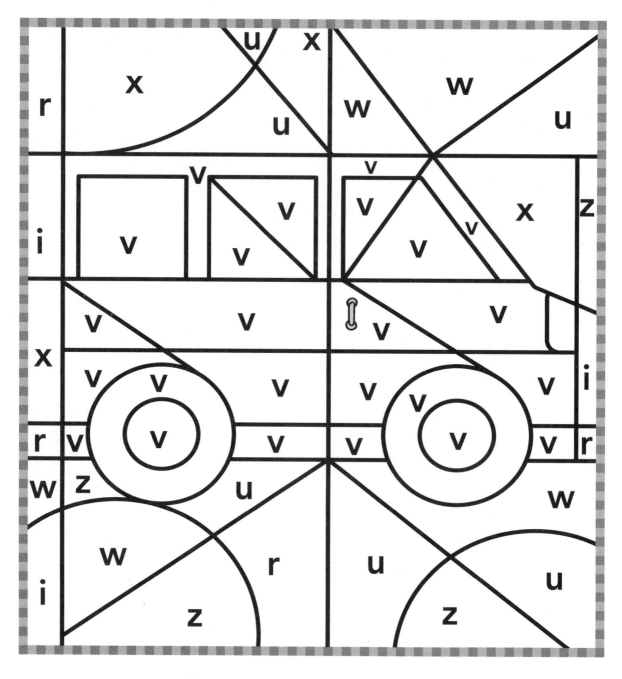

Circle the answer.

I made a  .

Write **V** to complete the word.

ulture

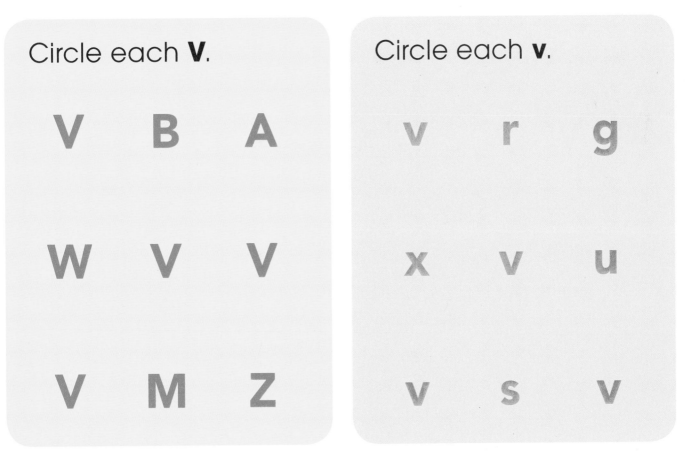

Circle each **V**.

V	B	A
W	V	V
V	M	Z

Circle each **v**.

v	r	g
x	v	u
v	s	v

Circle each **W** on the **WALRUS**.

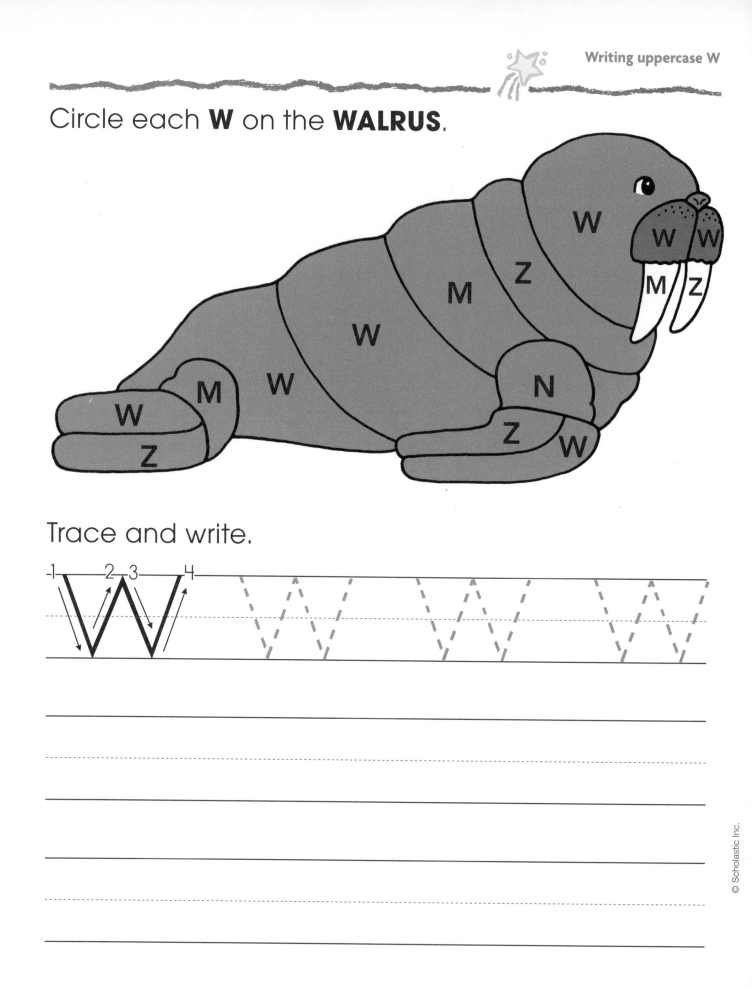

Trace and write.

Circle each item that begins with **W**.

Read the **w** words.

window   walrus

Trace and write.

1 2 3 4
W w w w w w

Trace each window pane. Write **w** on each one.

Find each **w**. Color that shape **blue**.

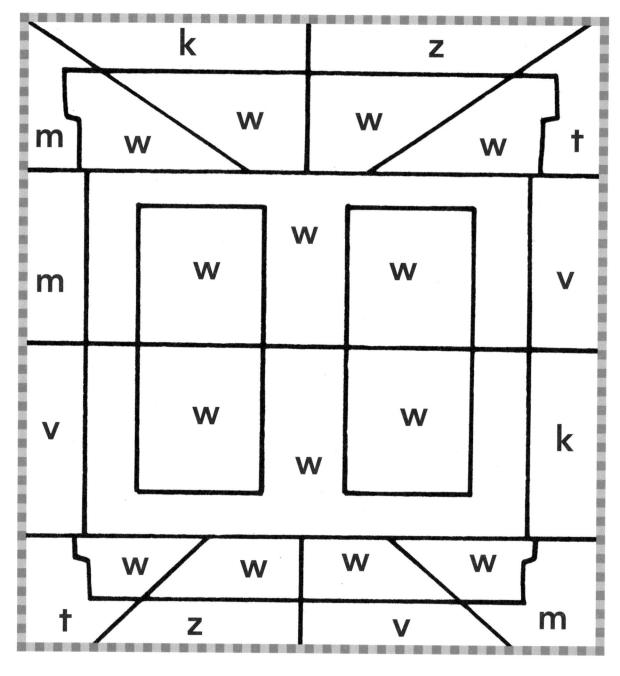

Circle the answer.

I made a   .

Write **W** to complete the word.

_altrus

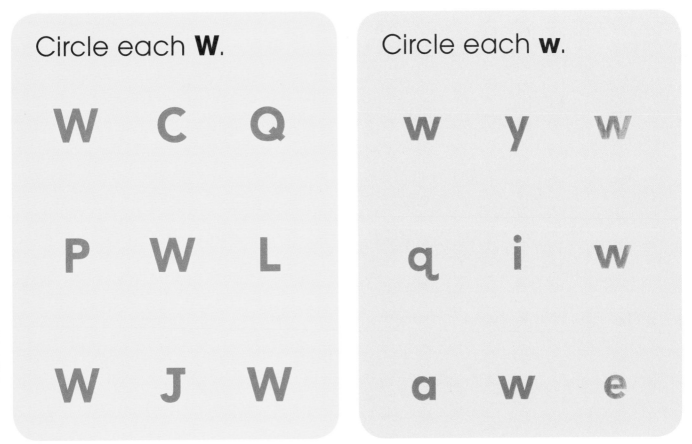

Circle each **W**.

W	C	Q
P	W	L
W	J	W

Circle each **w**.

w	y	w
q	i	w
a	w	e

Circle each **X** on the **X-RAY FISH**.

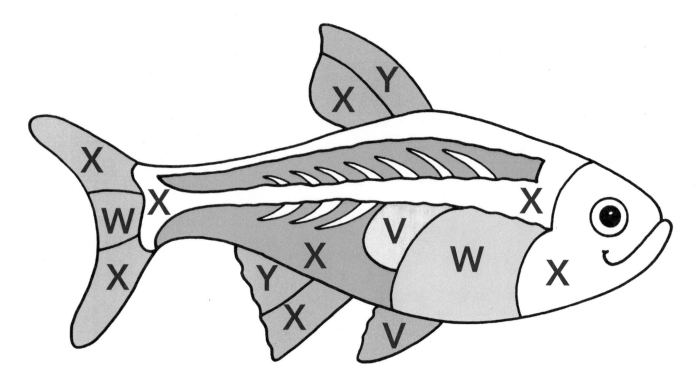

Trace and write.

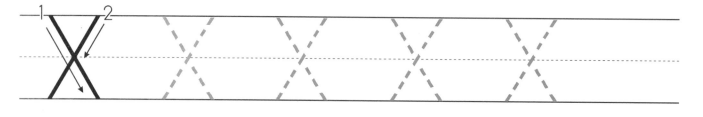

Circle each item that begins with **X** or has an **X** in it.

Read the **x** words.

x-ray fish

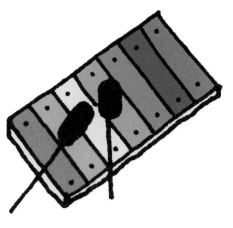

xylophone

Trace and write.

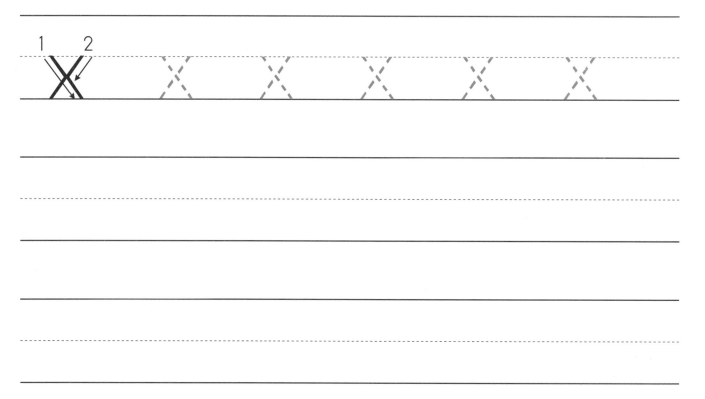

Trace each x-ray fish. Write **x** on each one.

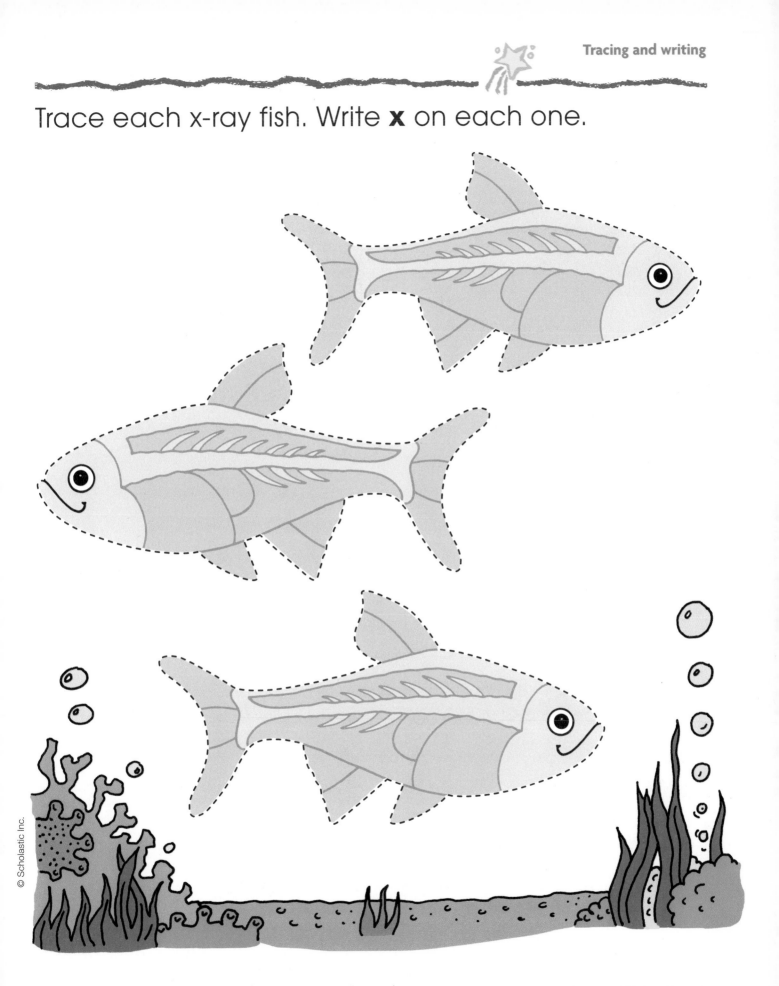

Find each **x**. Color that shape **yellow**.

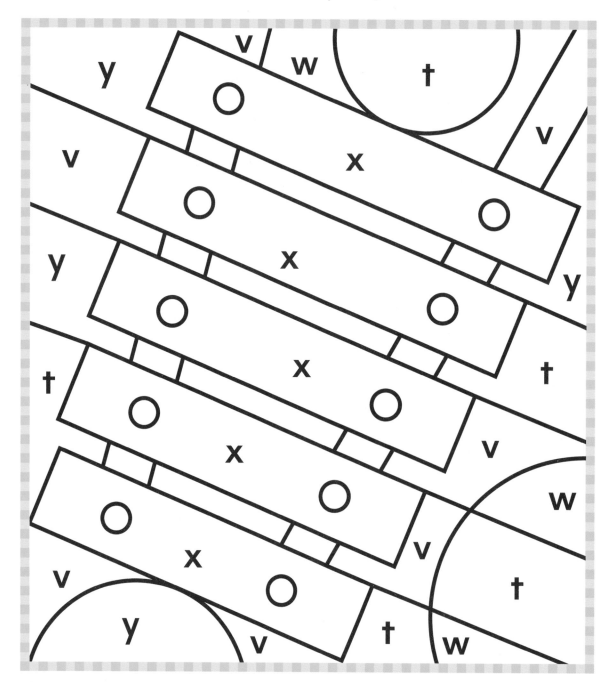

Circle the answer.

I made a  .

Write **X** to complete the word.

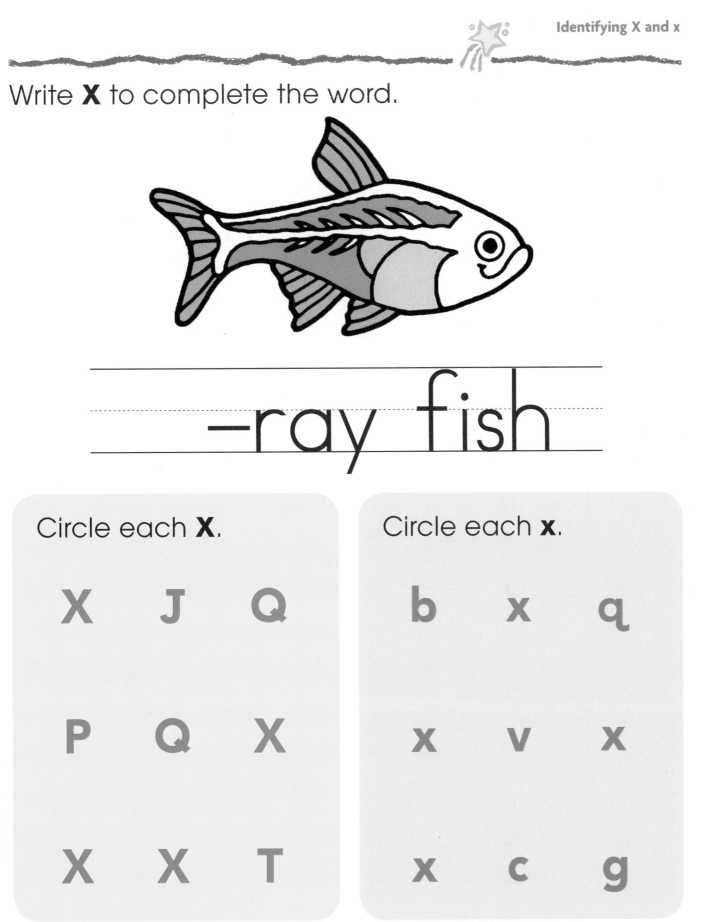

_____-ray fish

Circle each **X**.

X	J	Q
P	Q	X
X	X	T

Circle each **x**.

b	x	q
x	v	x
x	c	g

© Scholastic Inc.

Circle each **Y** on the **YAK**.

Trace and write.

Circle each item that begins with **Y**.

Read the **y** words.

yak

yo-yo

Trace and write.

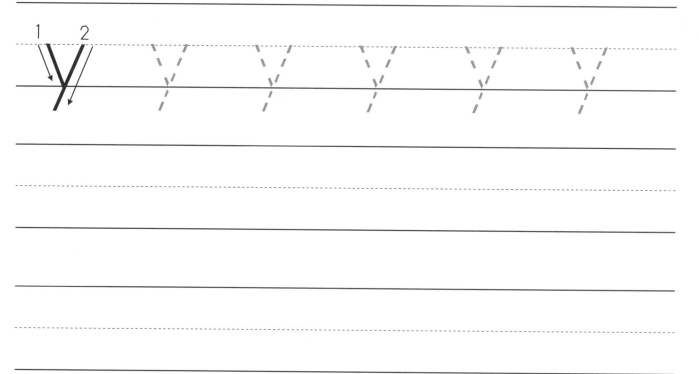

Trace each yo-yo. Write **y** on each one.

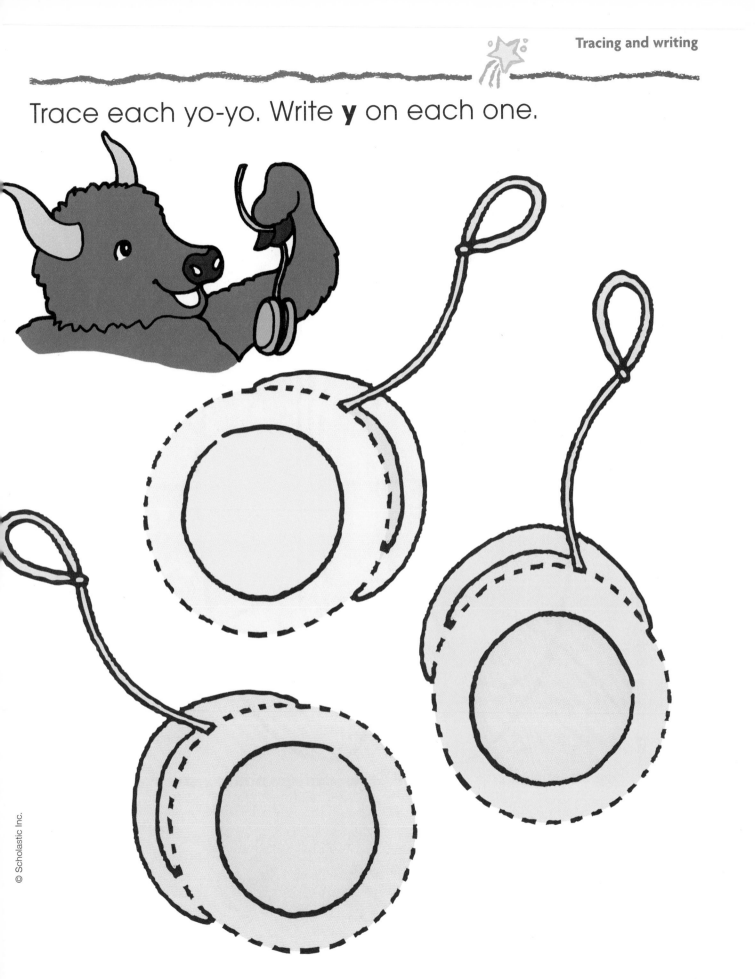

Find each **y**. Color that shape **green**.

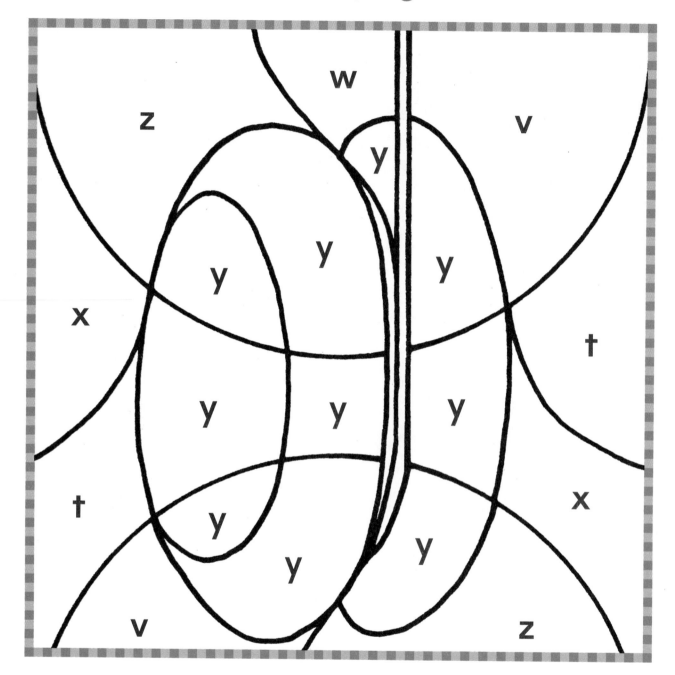

Circle the answer.

I made a  .

Write **Y** to complete the word.

Circle each **Y**.

N	Q	Y
P	Y	Y
J	T	Y

Circle each **y**.

y	r	y
u	e	b
y	y	p

Circle each **Z** on the **ZEBRA**.

Trace and write.

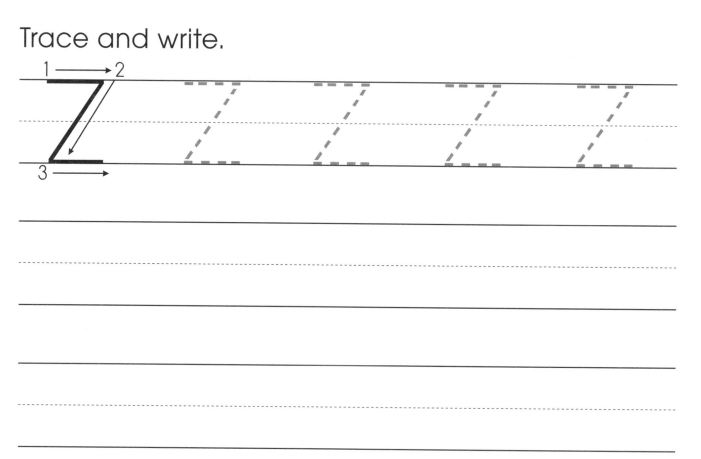

Circle each item that begins with **Z**.

Read the **z** words.

zebra

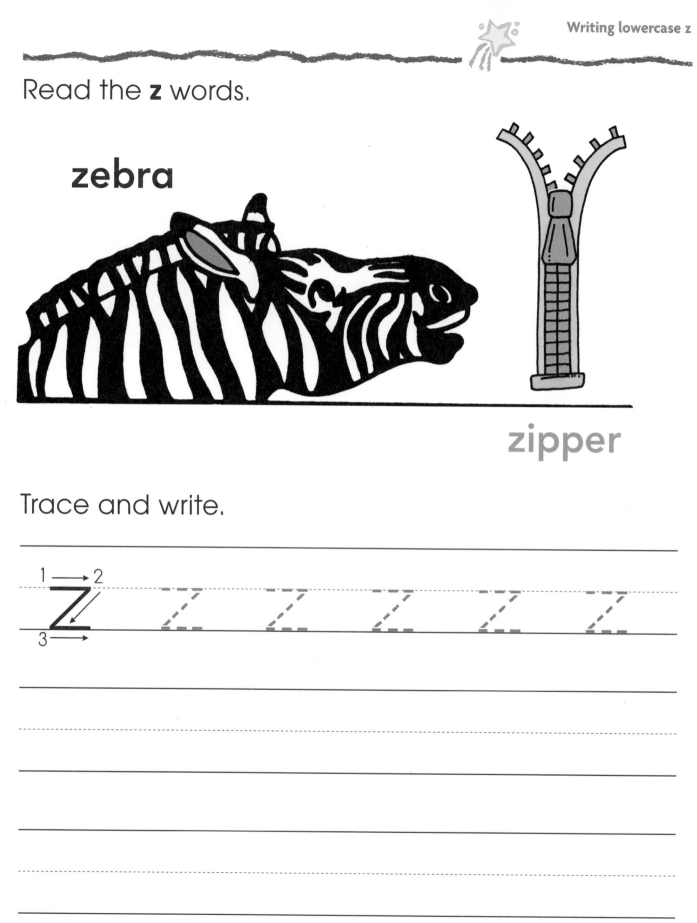

zipper

Trace and write.

Trace each zucchini. Write **z** on each one.

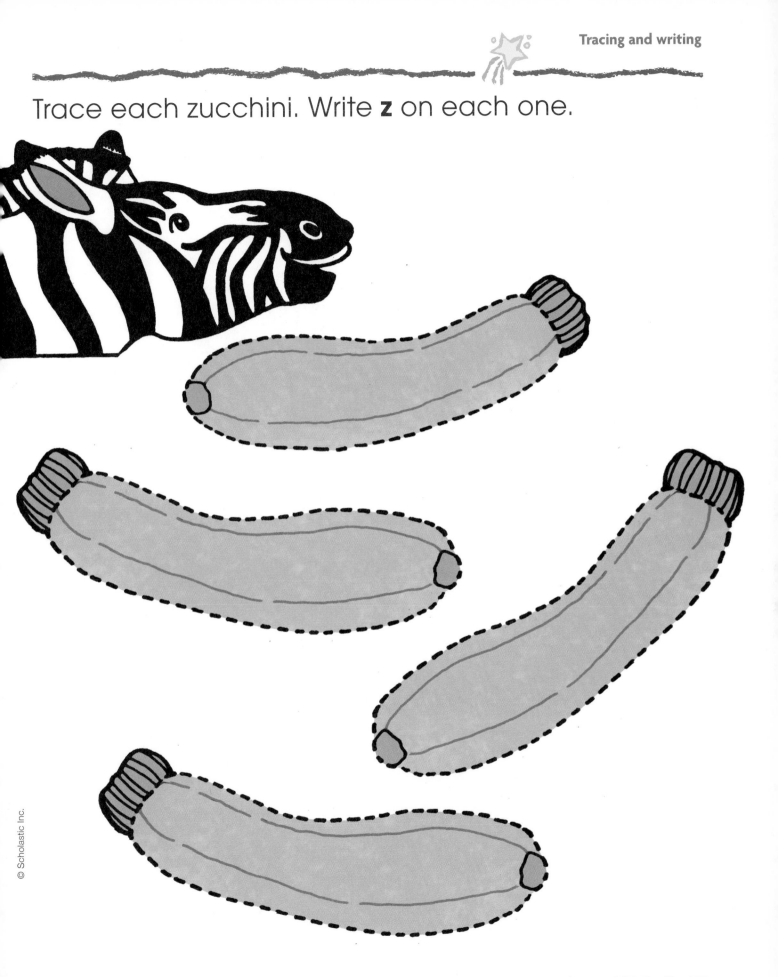

Find each **z**. Color that shape **purple**.

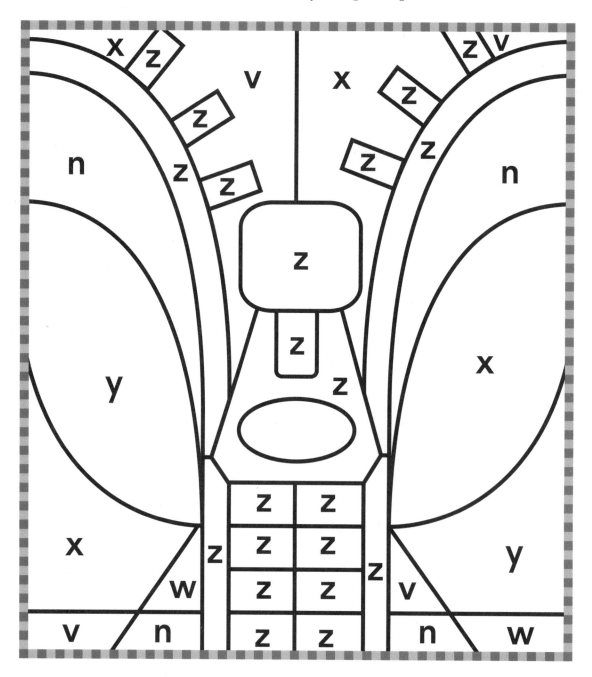

Circle the answer.

I made a  .

Write **Z** to complete the word.

_ebra

Circle each **Z**.

Y	Z	Z
Z	P	Q
J	Z	A

Circle each **z**.

z	z	j
s	z	i
i	z	m

Write your name.

Hello. My name is . . .

Color the boxes that show the different letters in your name.

NUMBERS

Trace the **I**.

I sun

Trace and write.

Circle **1** sun in each row.

1.

2.

3.

Circle each **1**.

one

Trace the **one**.

one bird

Trace and write.

one one one

How many suns? Write the number in the box.

Draw **1** sun in the sky.

© Scholastic Inc.

Trace the **2**.

 shoes

Trace and write.

Circle **2** shoes in each row.

1.

2.

3.

Circle each **2**.

2   1   2

2   1   4

3

2   3   2   4

2

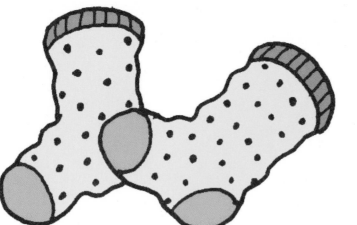

two

Trace the **two**.

two socks

Trace and write.

two   two   two

How many shoes? Write the number in the circle.

Draw **2** shoes in the shoebox.

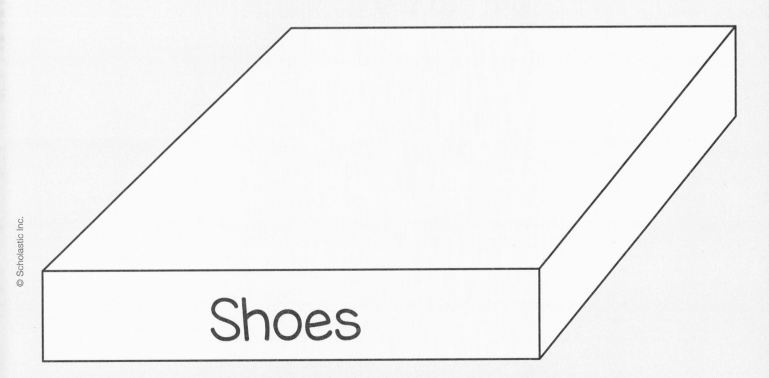

Shoes

Trace the **3**.

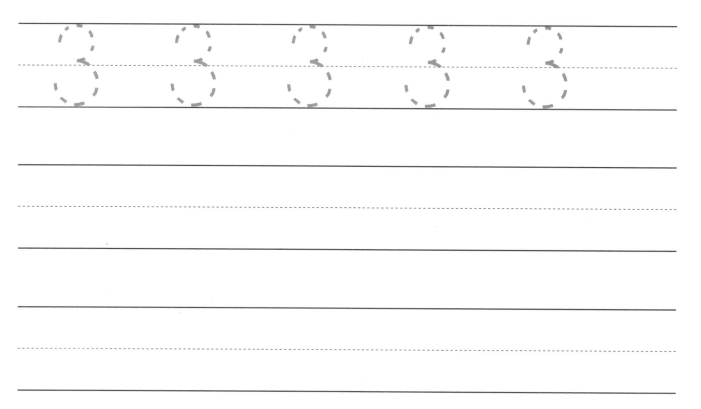

bees

Trace and write.

Circle **3** bees in each row.

1.

2.

3.

Circle each **3**.

2 3 3 4

4 1 2 1

3 3 3 1

Trace the **three**.

 jars

Trace and write.

How many bees? Write the number in the box.

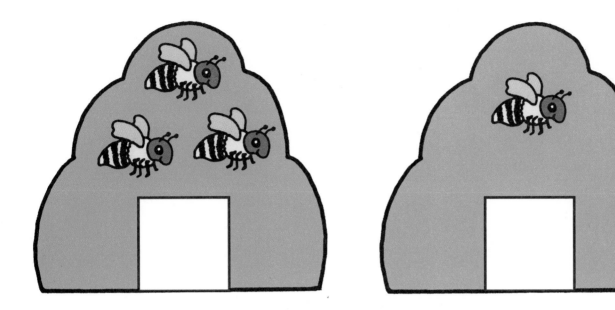

Draw **3** bees on the flower.

Trace the **4**.

4 ladybugs

Trace and write.

Circle **4** ladybugs in each row.

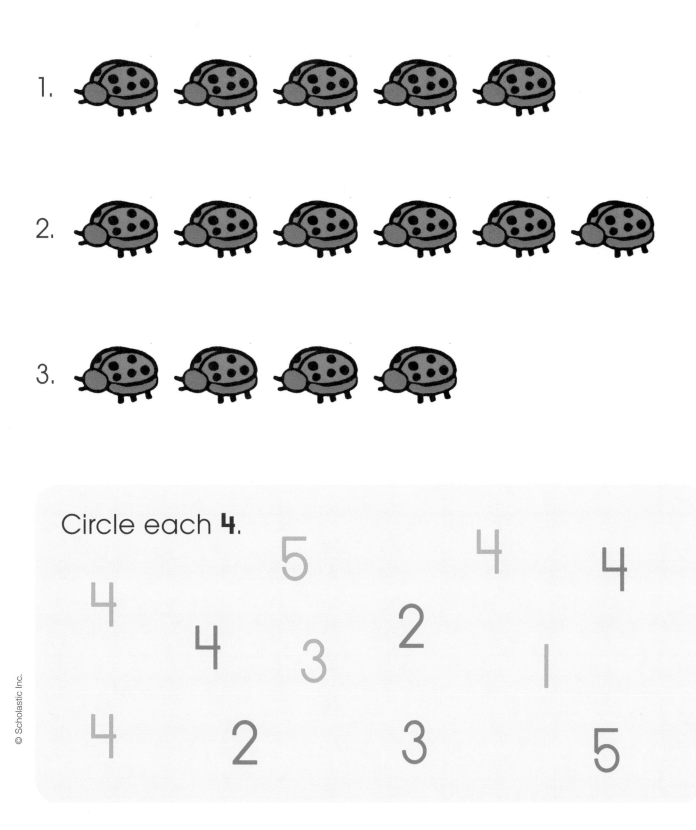

1.

2.

3.

Circle each **4**.

4 5 4 4

4 3 2

2 1

4 2 3 5

Trace the **four**.

four flowers

Trace and write.

How many ladybugs? Write the number on the line.

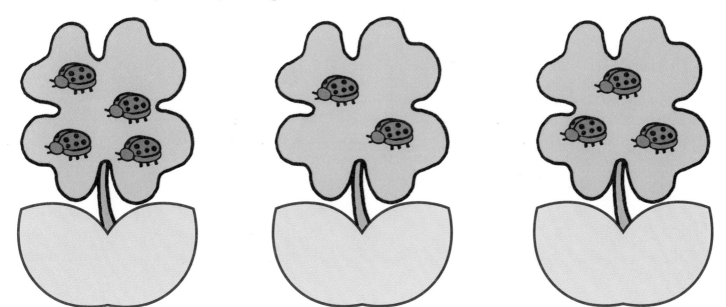

Draw **4** ladybugs on the leaf.

Trace the **5**.

 stars

Trace and write.

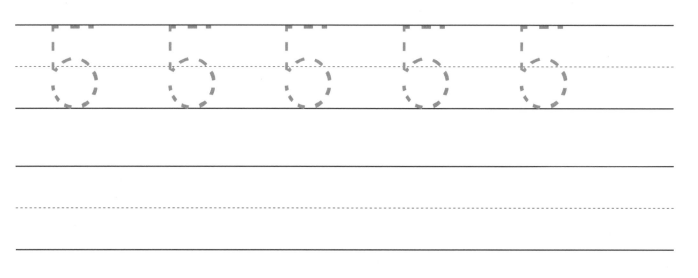

Circle **5** stars in each row.

1.  ☆ ☆ ☆ ☆ ☆ ☆ ☆

2.  ☆ ☆ ☆ ☆ ☆

3.  ☆ ☆ ☆ ☆ ☆ ☆

Circle each **5**.

5   3   5   3

1   5   1

4   5   2   5   4

Trace the **five**.

 planets

Trace and write.

How many stars? Write the number in the circle.

Draw **5** stars in the sky.

Trace the **6**.

 seeds

Trace and write.

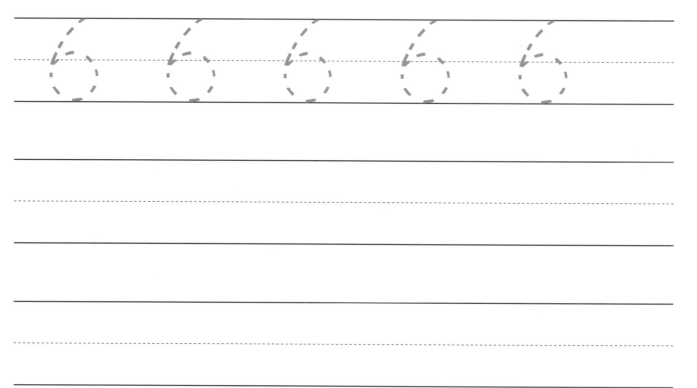

Circle **6** chicks in each row.

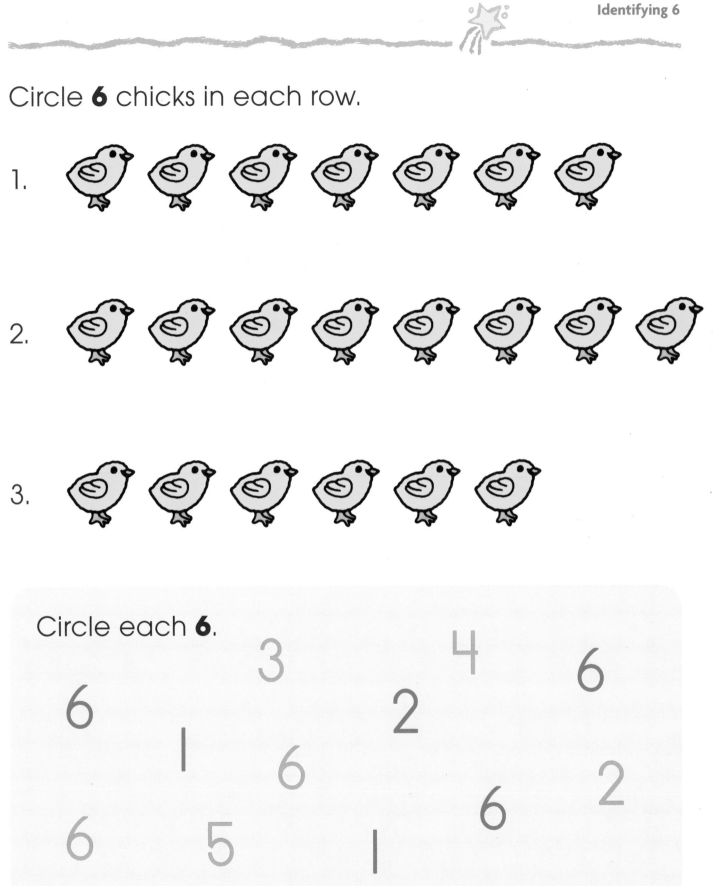

1.

2.

3.

Circle each **6**.

6   3   4
                    6
   1   2
        6
6   6   2

6   5   6
         1

Trace the **six**.

six eggs

Trace and write.

How many eggs? Write the number in the box.

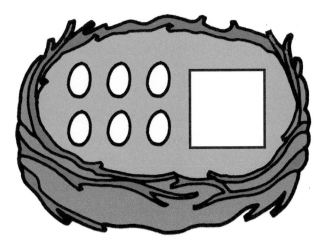 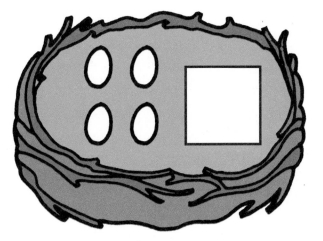

Draw **6** eggs in the nest.

Trace the **7**.

7 strawberries

Trace and write.

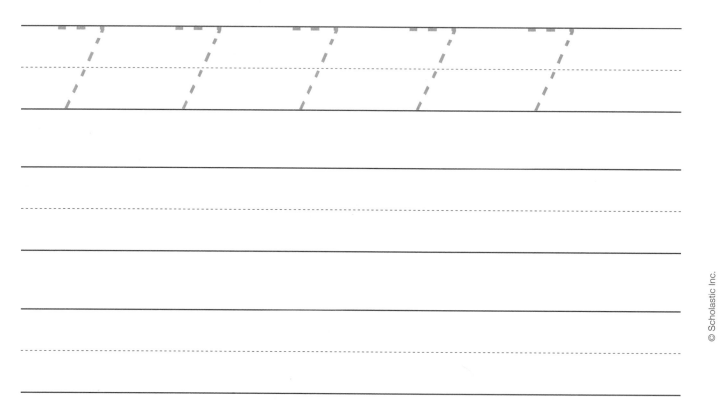

Circle **7** pieces of fruit.

Circle each **7**.

6   7   3

7

3   4   7   2

1   7   5   7

Trace the **seven**.

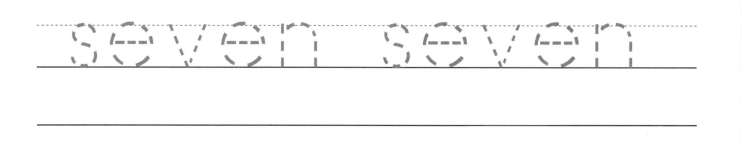

blueberries

Trace and write.

seven seven

How many strawberries?
Write the number in the box.

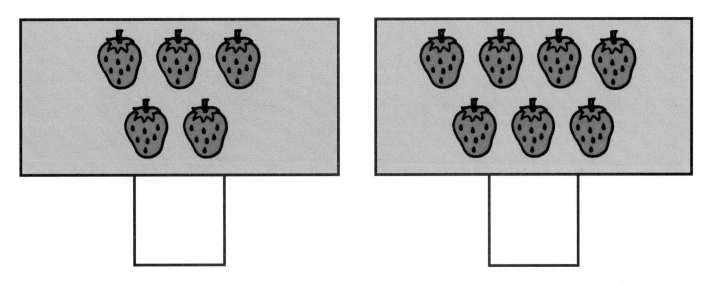

Draw **7** seeds on each strawberry.

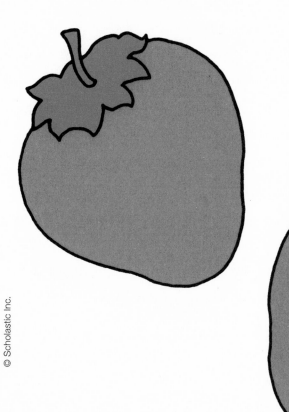

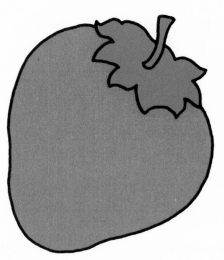

Trace the **8**.

cupcakes

Trace and write.

Circle **8** cupcakes.

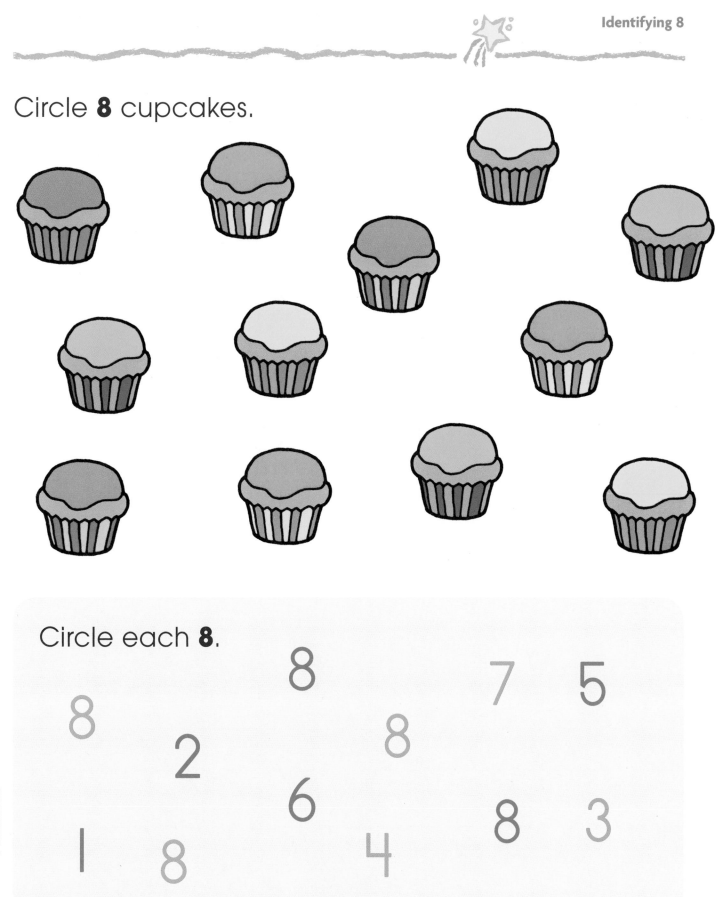

Circle each **8**.

8

8   7 5

8   8

2

6   8 3

1   8   4

eight

Trace the **eight**.

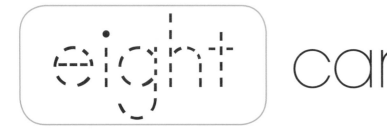 candies

Trace and write.

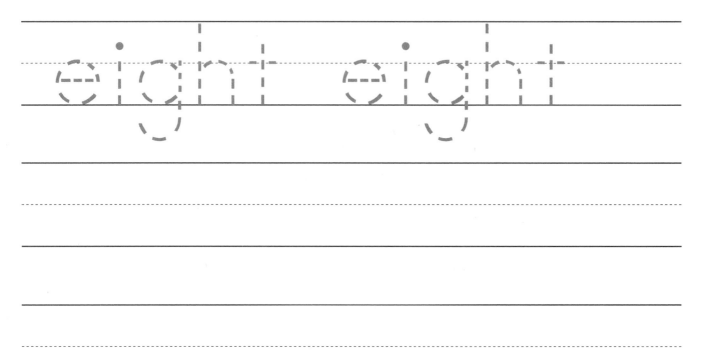

How many candies? Write the number in the box.

Draw **8** candies on the cupcake.

Trace the **9**.

9 butterflies

Trace and write.

Circle **9** creepy crawlies.

Circle each **9**.

q   q   4   q

q

2   5   6   1

8   q   q   3

nine

Trace the **nine**.

nine caterpillars

Trace and write.

nine nine

How many spots? Write the number in the box.

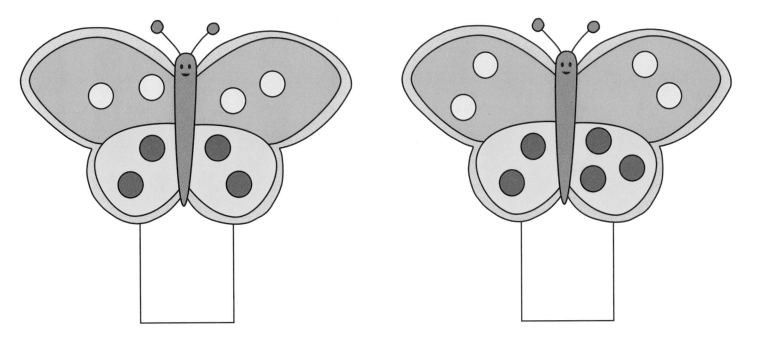

Draw **9** spots on the butterfly.

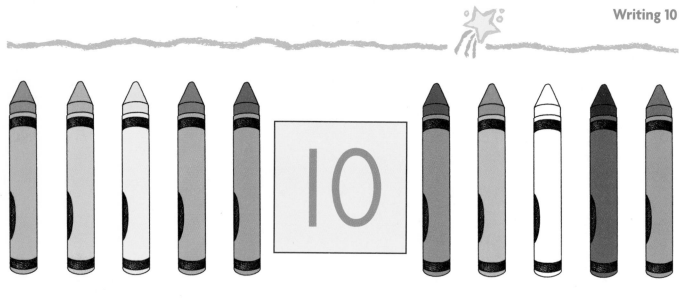

Trace the **10**.

 crayons

Trace and write.

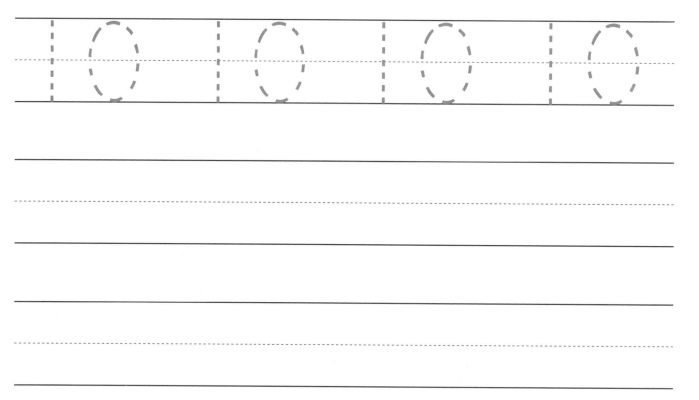

Circle **10** smiley faces.

Circle each **10**.

10   4   10   9

10   6   10   10   10

3   1   2   3

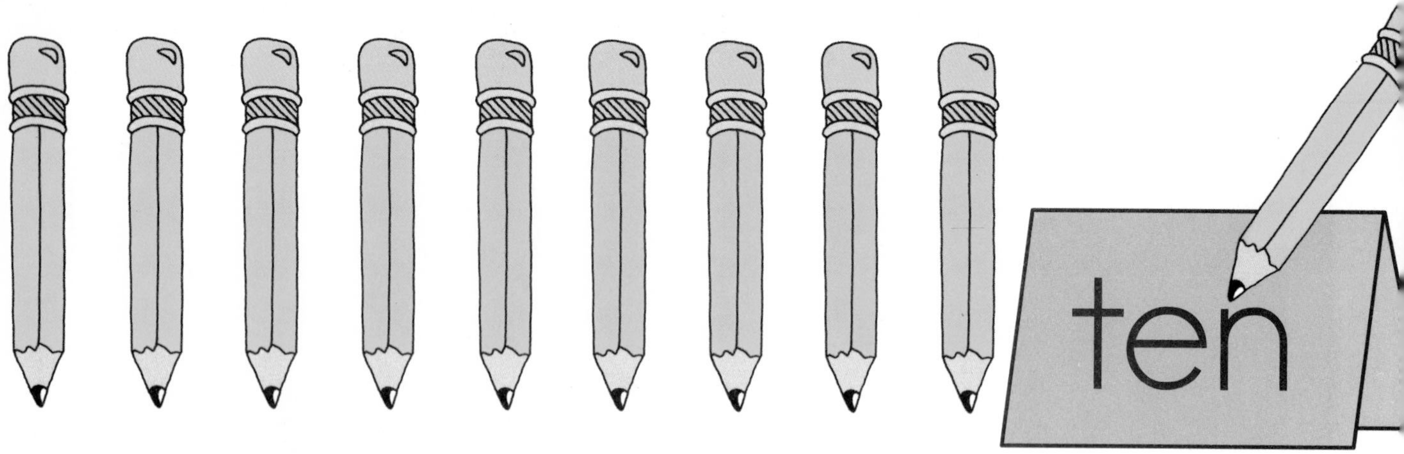

Trace the **ten**.

ten pencils

Trace and write.

ten ten ten

How many crayons? Write the number in the box.

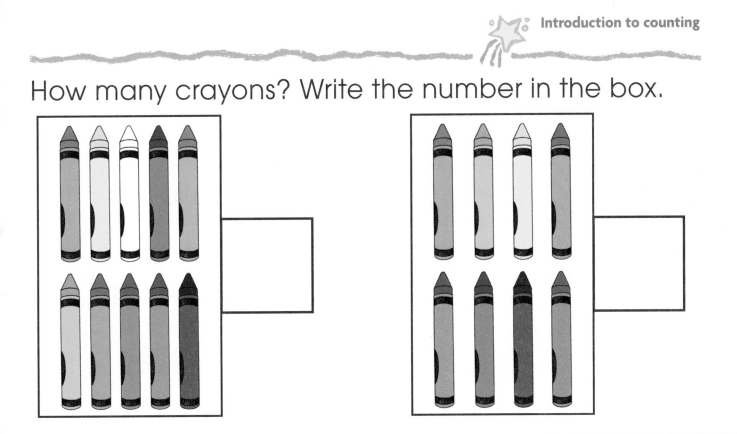

Draw **10** crayons in the box.

Write your name.

Hello. My name is . . .

Count the number of letters in your name.
Color the box that shows that number.

1	2	3	4
5	6	7	8
9	10	more than 10	

COLORS AND SHAPES

This apple is **red**. Color the second apple **red**.

Trace and write.

red red red

Circle the things that are **red**.

Count the things that are **red**.

I circled _____ things!

number

This bird is **blue**. Color the second bird **blue**.

Trace and write.

Circle the things that are **blue**.

Count the things that are **blue**.

I circled _____ things!
number

This bus is **yellow**. Color the second bus **yellow**.

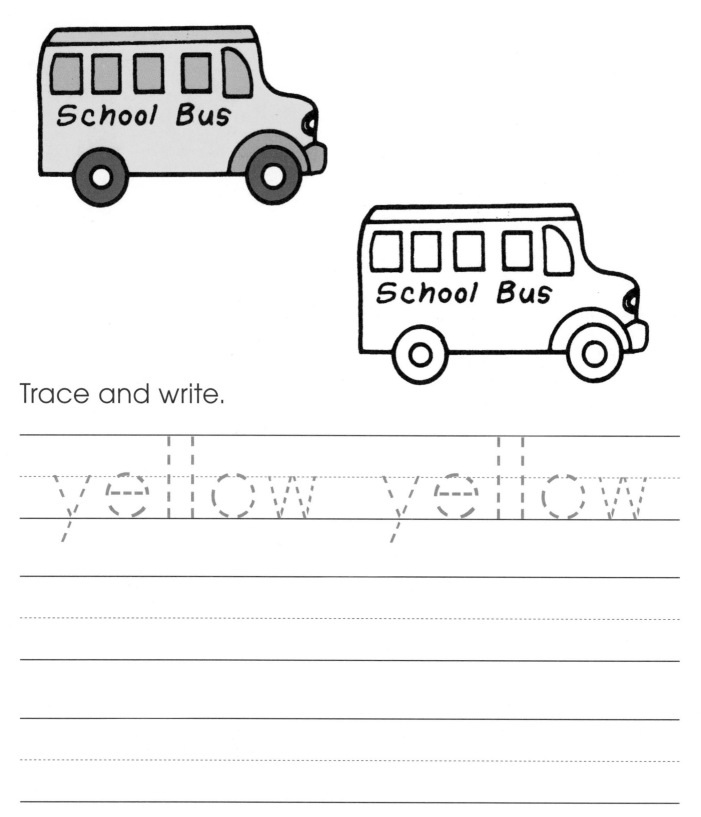

Trace and write.

yellow yellow

Circle the things that are yellow.

Count the things that are yellow.

I circled _____ things!
number

This frog is **green**. Color the second frog **green**.

Trace and write.

green   green

Circle the things that are **green**.

Count the things that are **green**.

I circled _____ things!
number

This pumpkin is **orange**.
Color the second pumpkin **orange**.

Trace and write.

orange   orange

Circle the things that are **orange**.

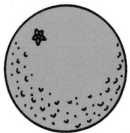

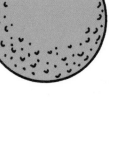

Count the things that are **orange**.

I circled _____ things!

number

This bunch of grapes is **purple**.
Color the second bunch of grapes **purple**.

Trace and write.

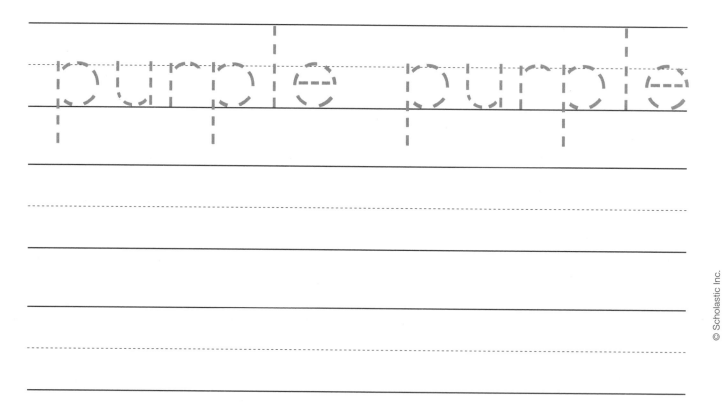

Circle the things that are **purple**.

Count the things that are **purple**.

I circled _____ things!

number

This pig is **pink**. Color the second pig **pink**.

Trace and write.

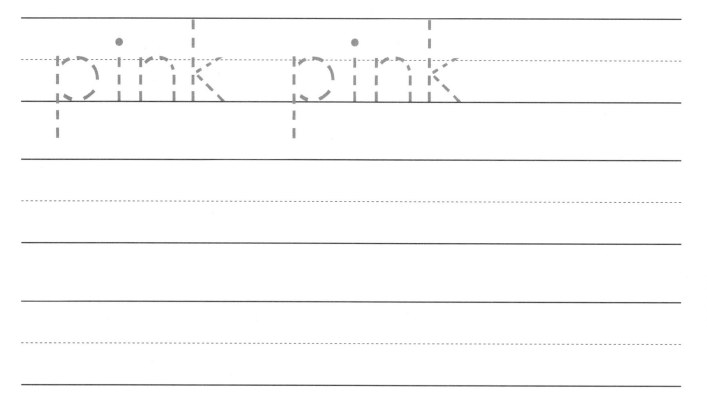

Circle the things that are **pink**.

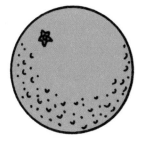

Count the things that are **pink**.

I circled _____ things!
number

This bear is **brown**. Color the second bear **brown**.

Trace and write.

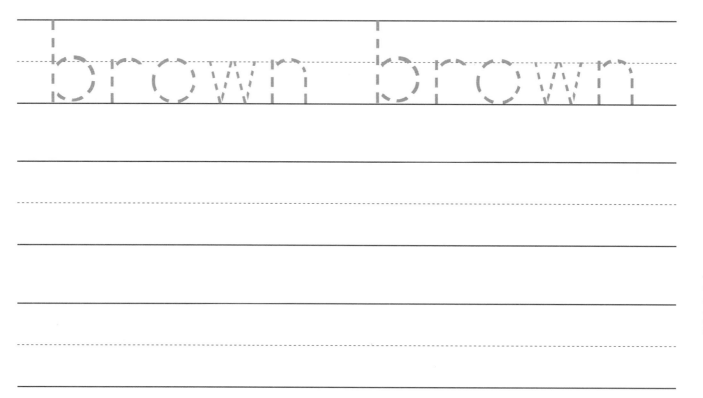

Circle the things that are **brown**.

School Bus

Count the things that are **brown**.

I circled _____ things!
number

This cat is **white**. Color the other cat a different color.

Trace and write.

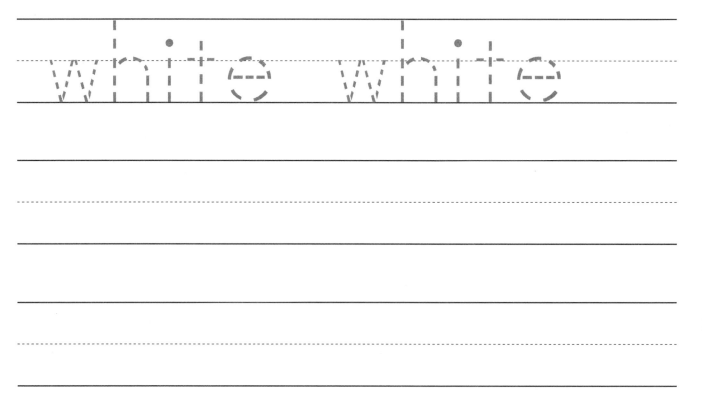

Circle the things that are white.

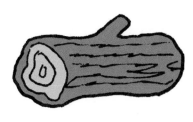

Count the things that are white.

I circled _____ things!
number

This bat is **black**. Color the second bat **black**.

Trace and write.

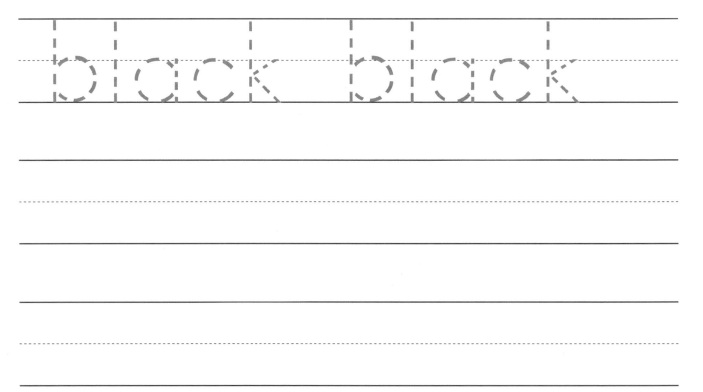

Circle the things that are **black**.

Count the things that are **black**.

I circled _____ things!
number

Use the color key to color the picture.

Color Key

red   yellow   green   blue

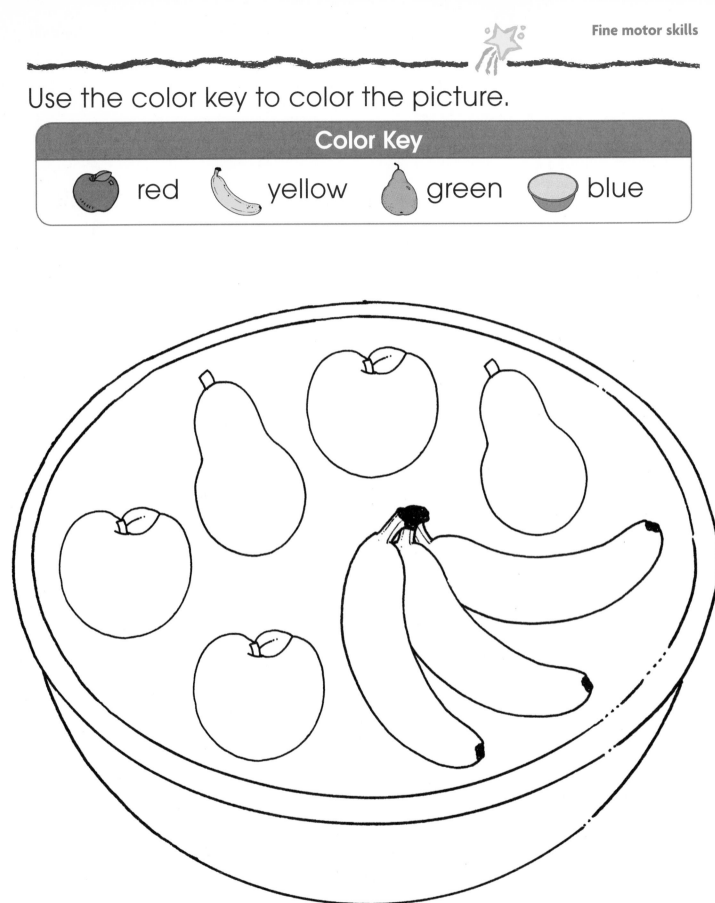

Use the color key to color the picture.

Use the color key to color the picture.

Color Key

red   blue   black   green

orange   purple   brown

Use the color key to color the picture.

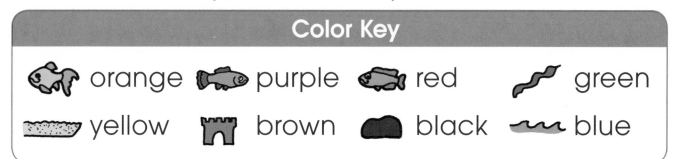

Color Key

orange   purple   red   green

yellow   brown   black   blue

Use the color key to color the picture.

Color Key

1 = 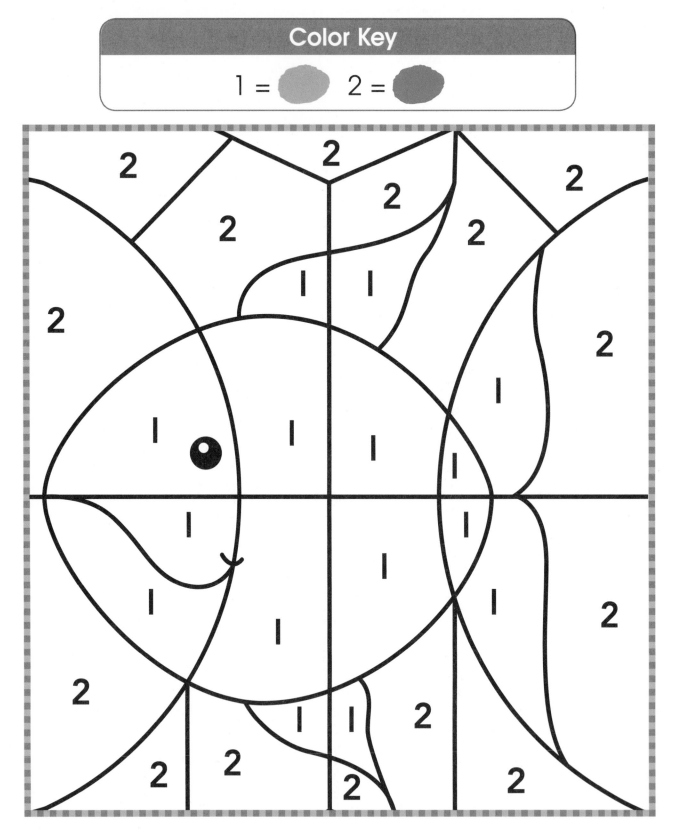 2 =

Use the color key to color the picture.

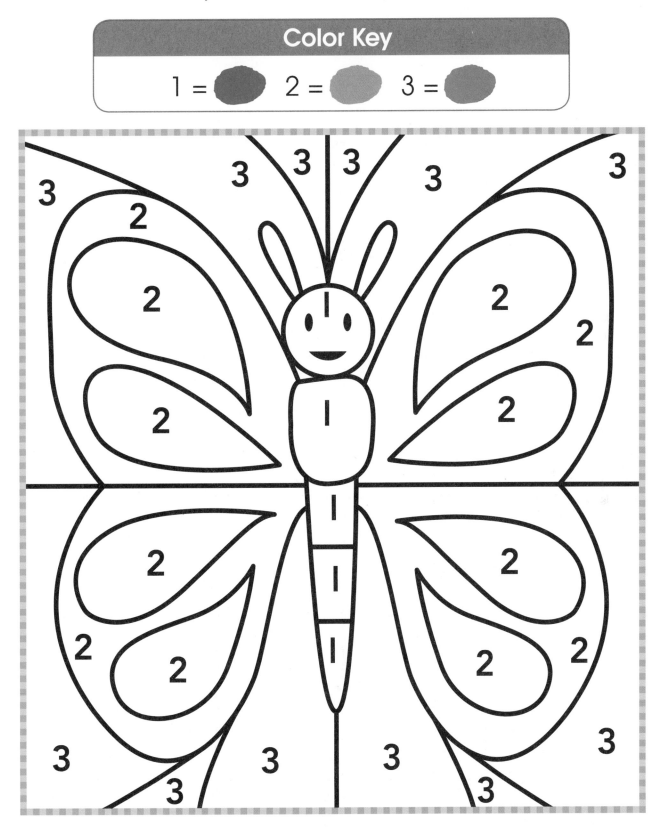

Use the color key to color the picture.

Use the color key to color the picture.

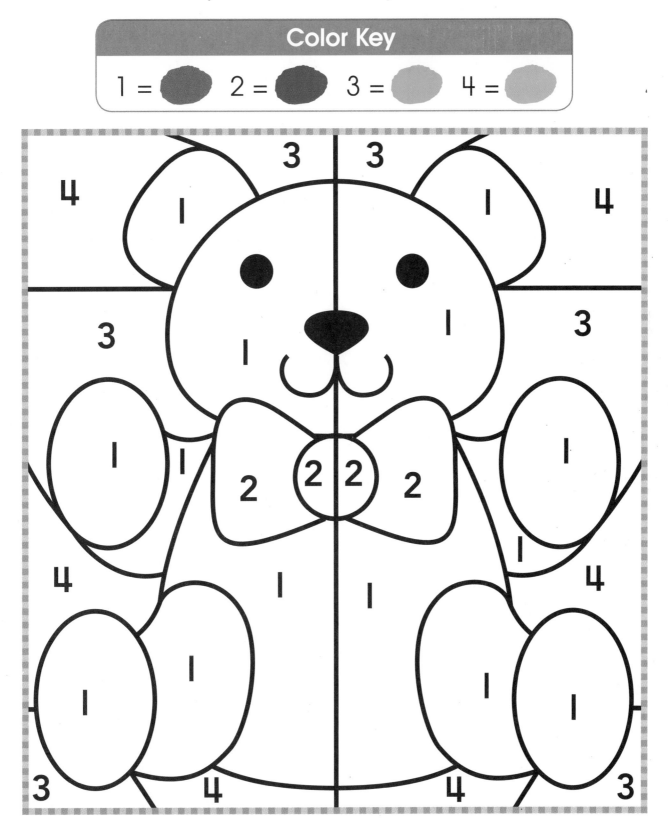

Use the words in the box to write the color for each picture.

| blue | green | white | yellow | red |

Use the words in the box to write the color for each picture.

| purple | pink | **black** | brown | orange |

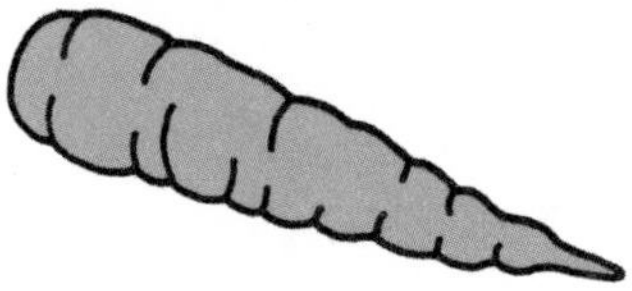

Draw a line to match each crayon to the animal of the same color.

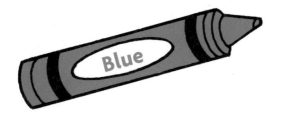

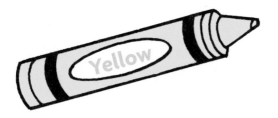

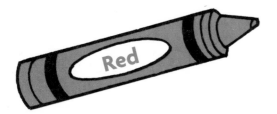

Draw a line to match each crayon to the animal of the same color.

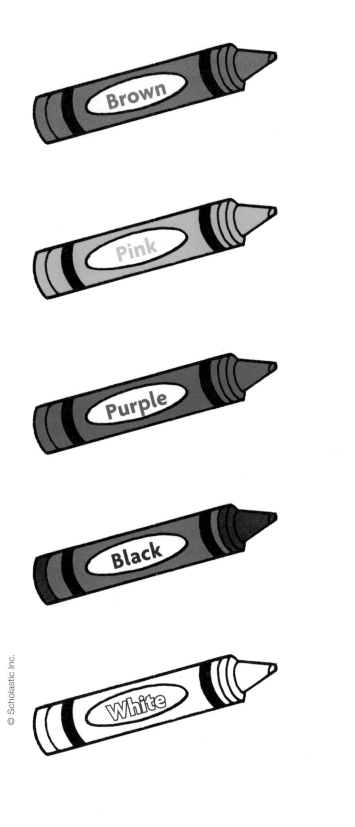

Count the **circles**.

This bug has _____ circles.
number

Trace each **circle**.

Draw a smiley face on each **circle**.

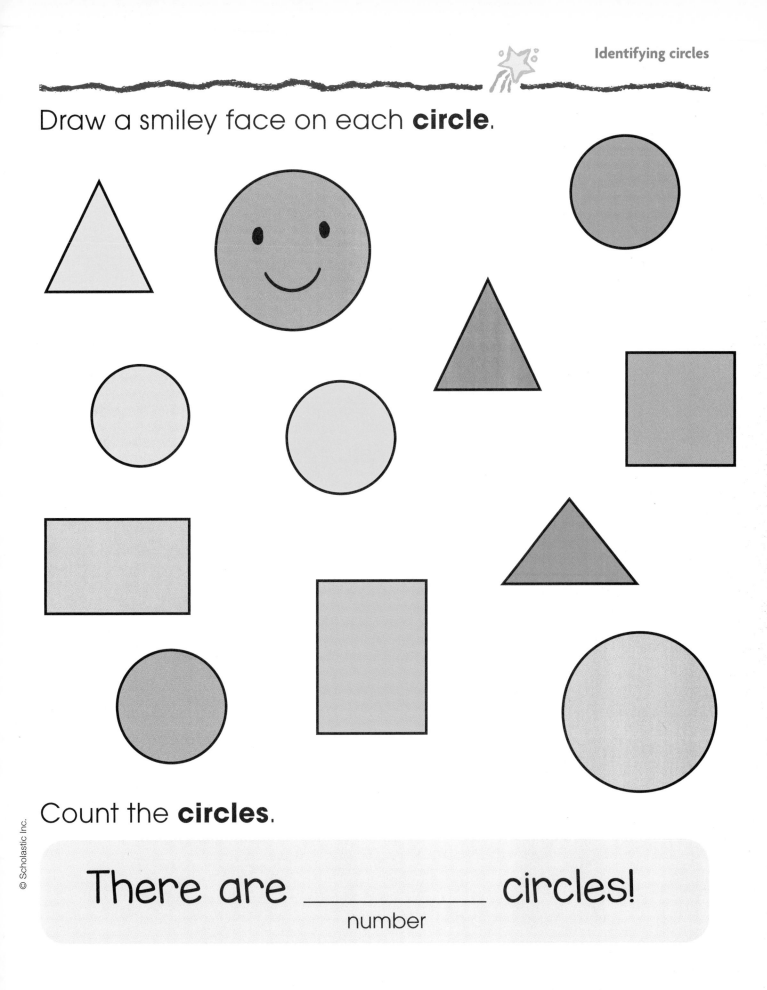

Count the **circles**.

There are _____ circles!
number

Trace each **circle**.

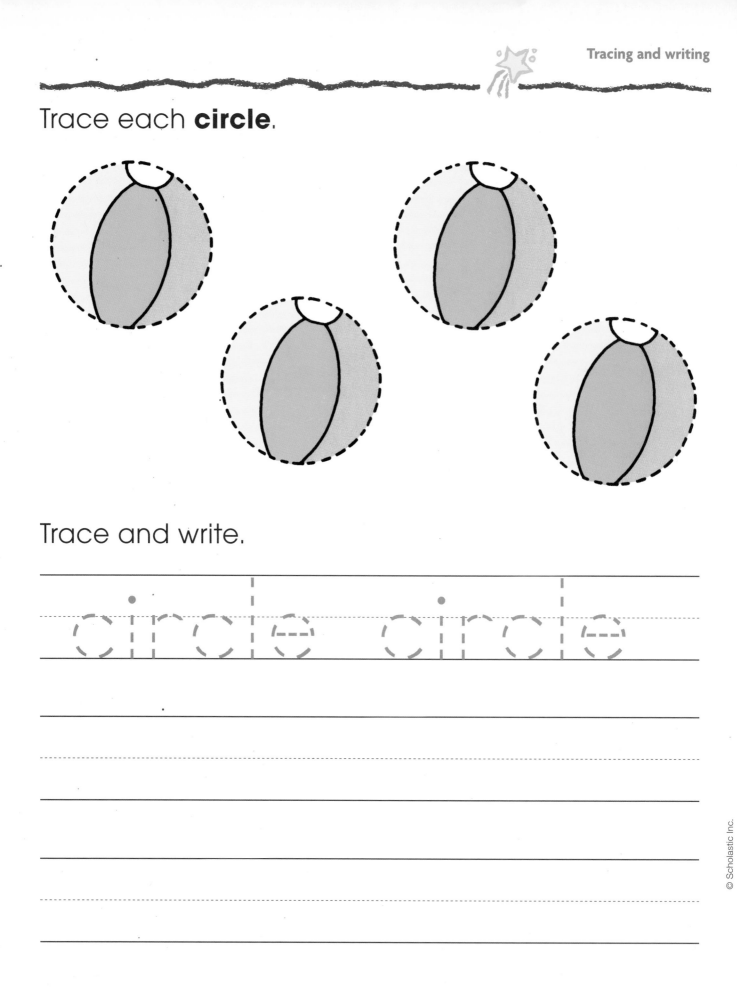

Trace and write.

circle circle

Draw balls on the beach. Make a ◯ for each ball.

Count the **squares**.

This quilt has _____ squares.

number

Trace each **square**.

Draw a smiley face on each **square**.

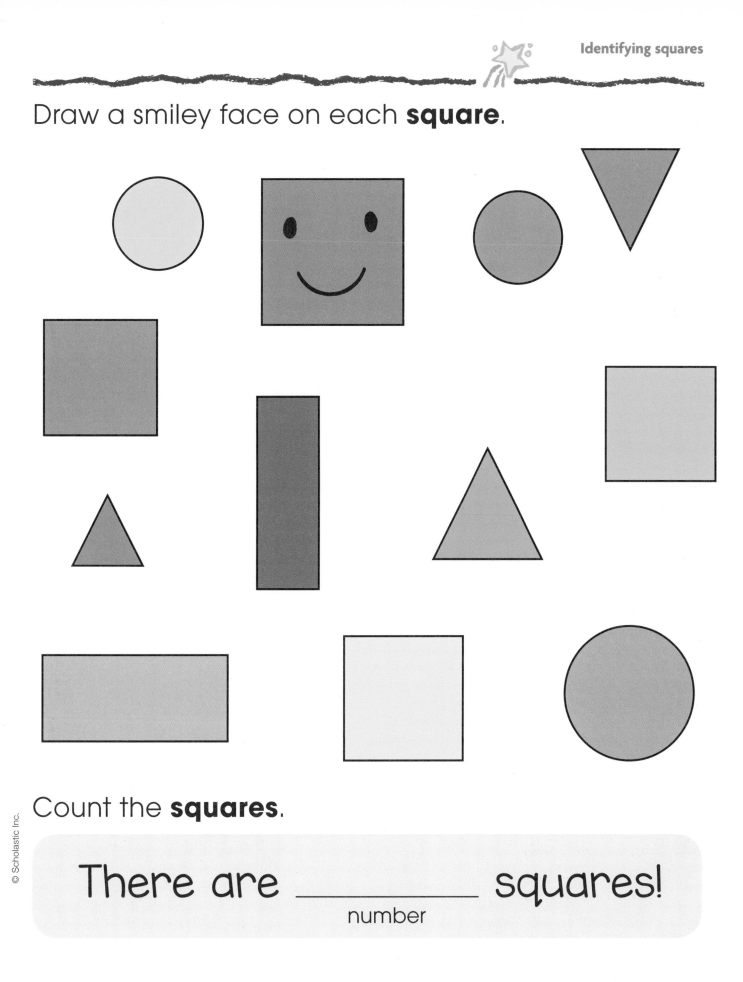

Count the **squares**.

There are _____ squares!
number

Trace each **square**.

Trace and write.

square

Draw windows on the house. Make a ☐ for each window.

Count the **triangles**.

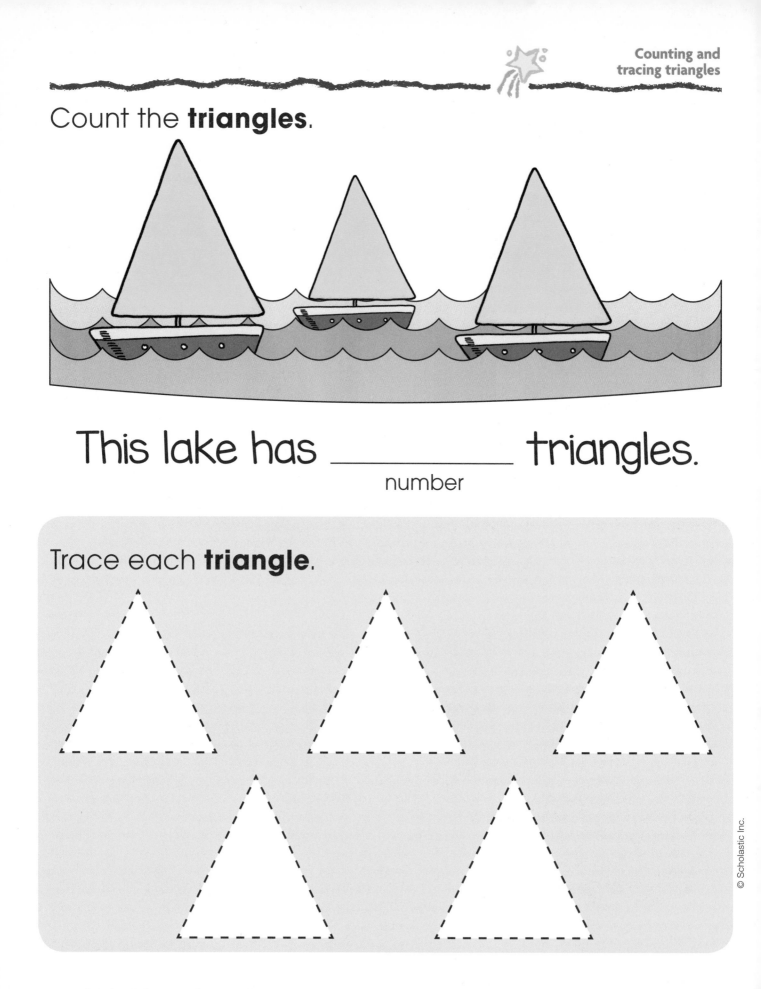

This lake has _____ triangles.
number

Trace each **triangle**.

Draw a smiley face on each **triangle**.

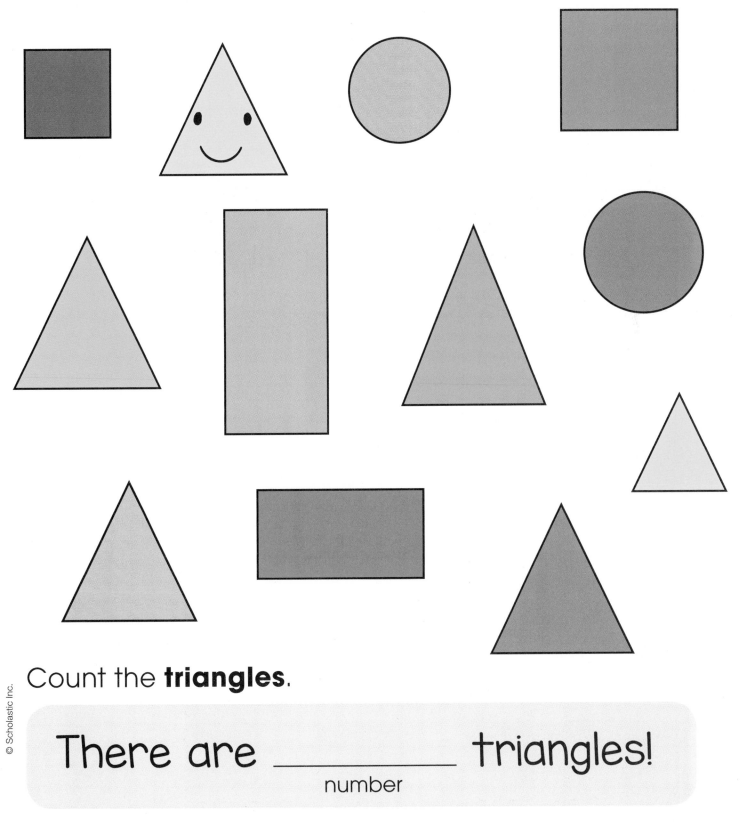

Count the **triangles**.

There are _____ triangles!

number

Trace each **triangle**.

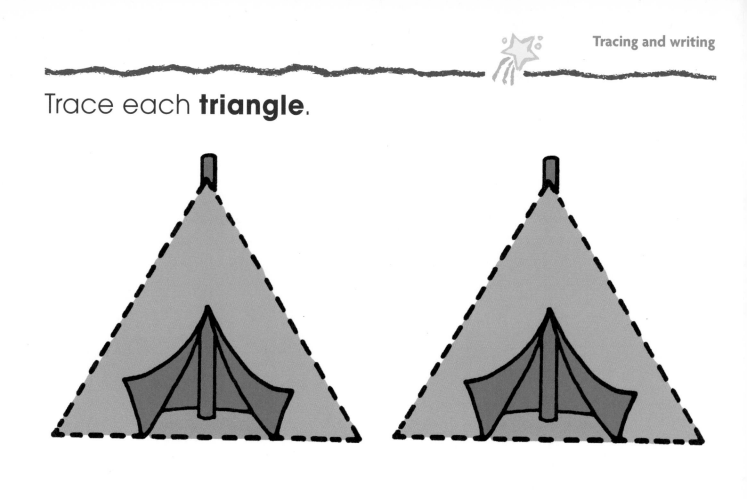

Trace and write.

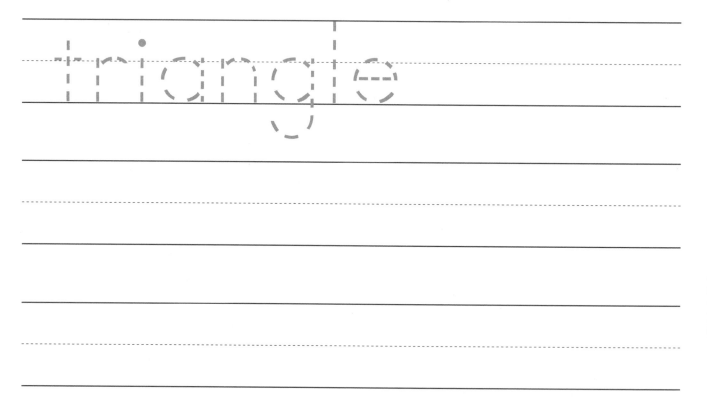

Draw tents at the campsite. Make a △ for each tent.

Count the **rectangles**.

This train has _____ rectangles.
number

Trace each **rectangle**.

Draw a smiley face on each **rectangle**.

Count the **rectangles**.

There are _____ rectangles!
number

Trace each **rectangle**.

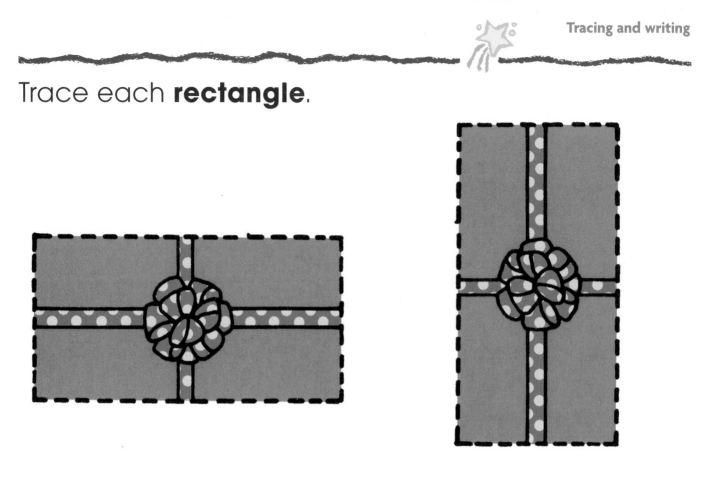

Trace and write.

Draw gifts at the party. Make a ☐ for each gift.

Count the **ovals**.

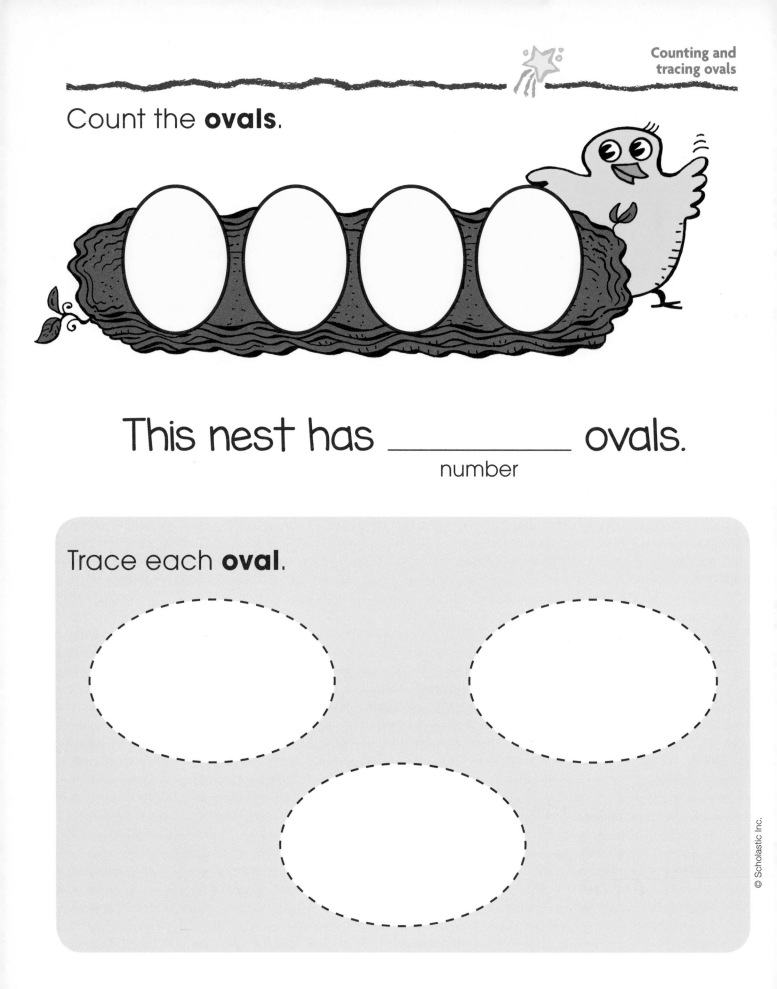

This nest has _____ ovals.

number

Trace each **oval**.

Draw a smiley face on each **oval**.

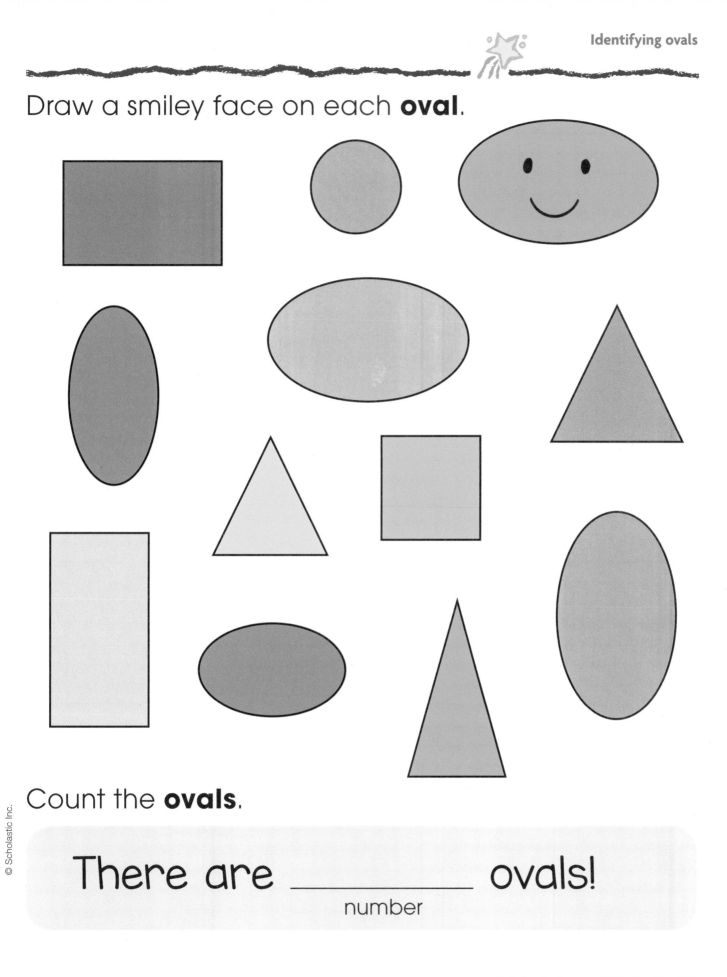

Count the **ovals**.

There are _____ ovals!
number

Trace each **oval**.

Trace and write.

Draw eggs in the nest. Make an $\bigcirc$ for each egg.

Count the **diamonds**.

This picture has _____ diamonds.
number

Trace each **diamond**.

Draw a smiley face on each **diamond**.

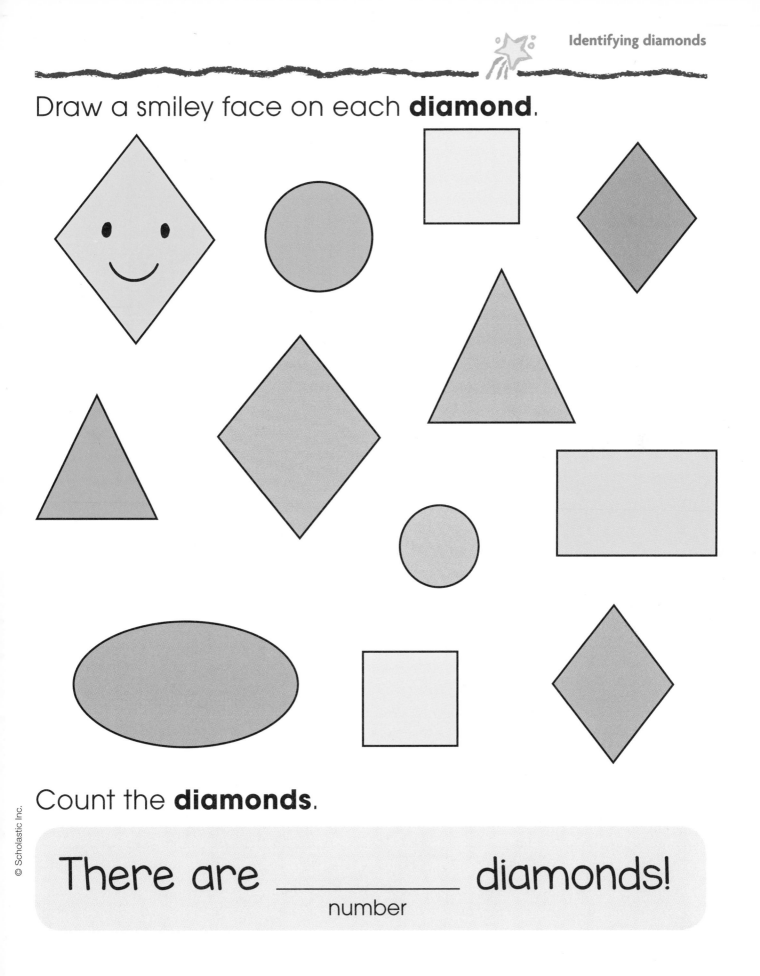

Count the **diamonds**.

There are _____ diamonds!
number

Trace each **diamond**.

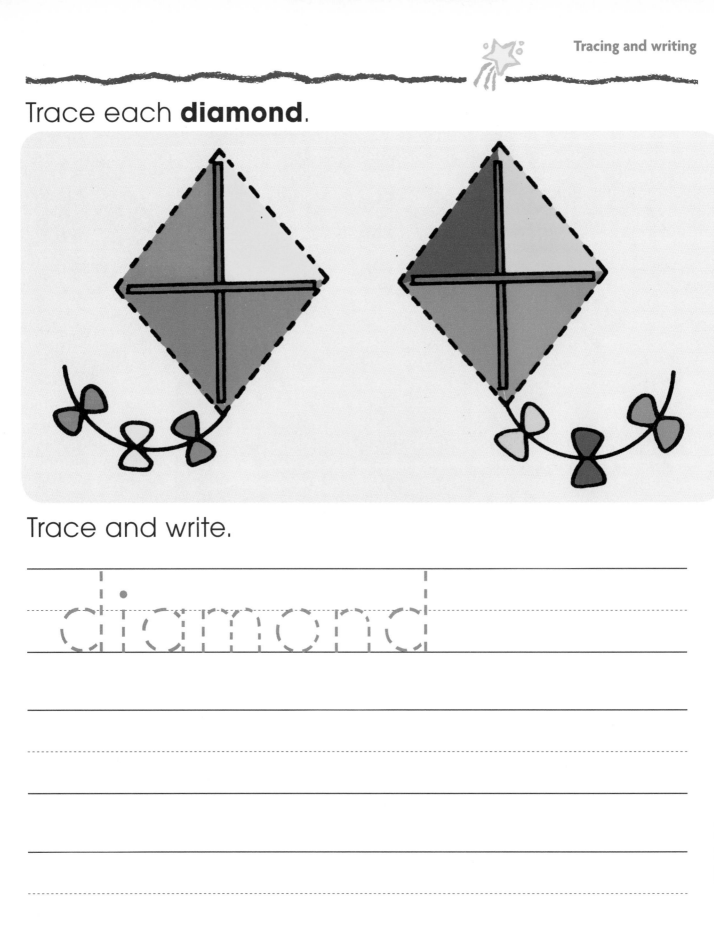

Trace and write.

diamond

Draw kites in the sky. Draw a ◇ for each kite.

Count the **stars** in the picture.

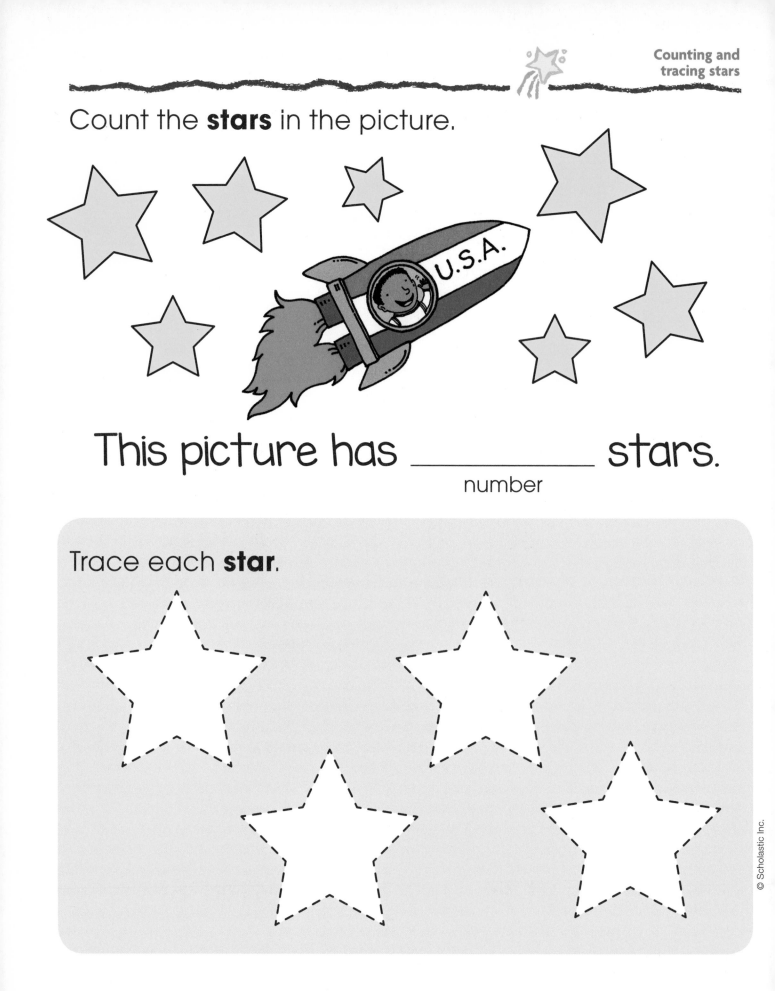

This picture has _____ stars.

number

Trace each **star**.

Draw a smiley face on each **star**.

Count the **stars**.

There are _____ stars!
number

Trace each **star**.

Trace and write.

star star

Draw stars in the sky. Make a ☆ for each star.

Count the **octagons** in the picture.

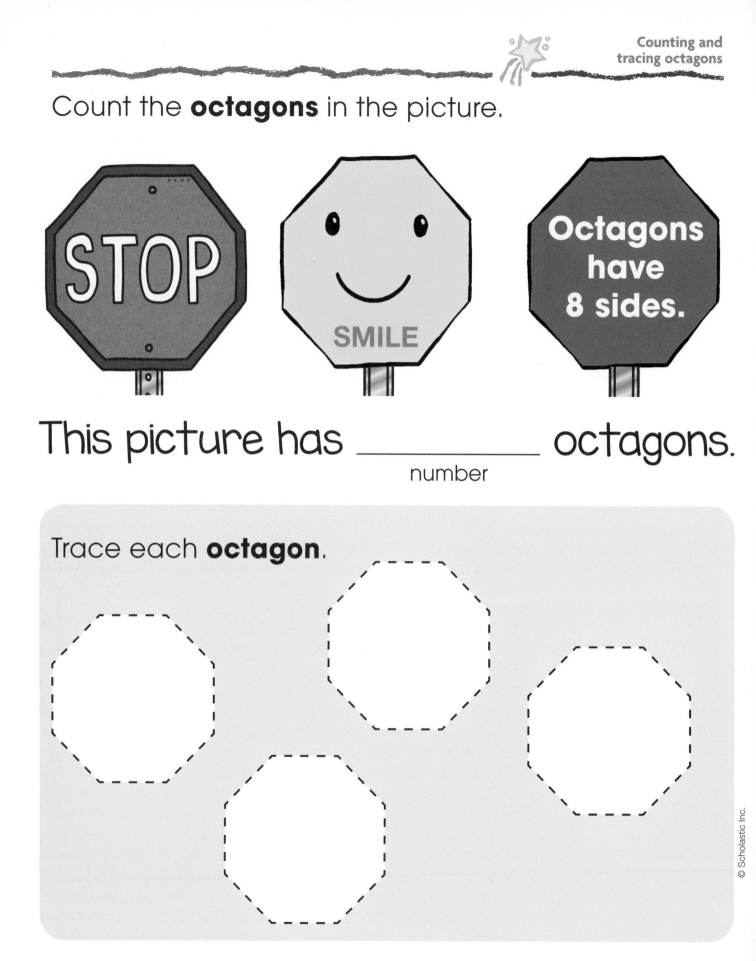

STOP

SMILE

Octagons
have
8 sides.

This picture has _____ octagons.
number

Trace each **octagon**.

Draw a smiley face on each **octagon**.

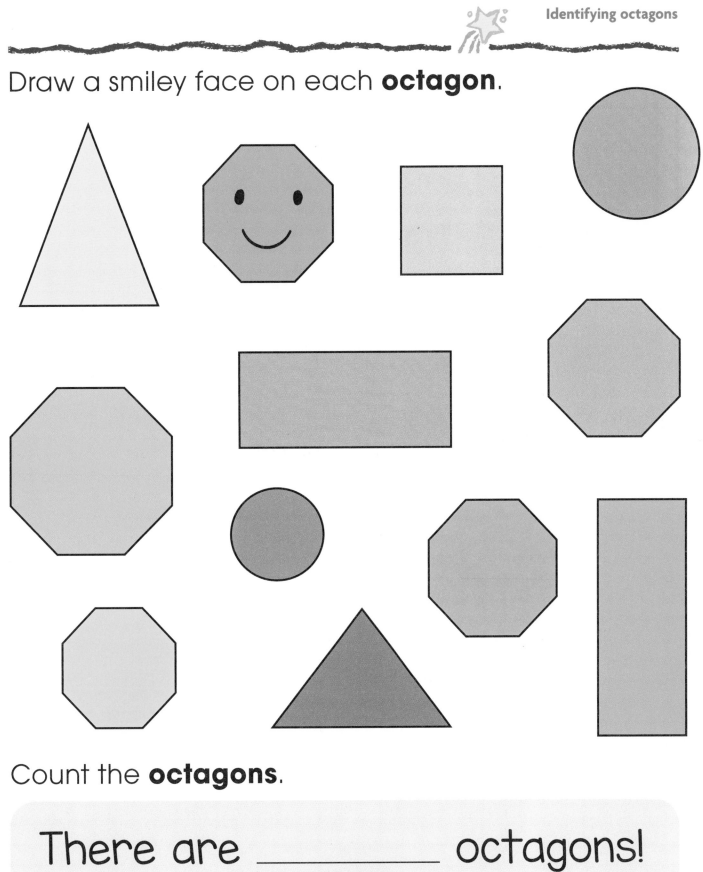

Count the **octagons**.

There are _____ octagons!
number

Trace each **octagon**.

Trace and write.

Trace an ⬡ on the sign post to make an octagon. Then draw a picture on it.

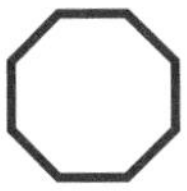

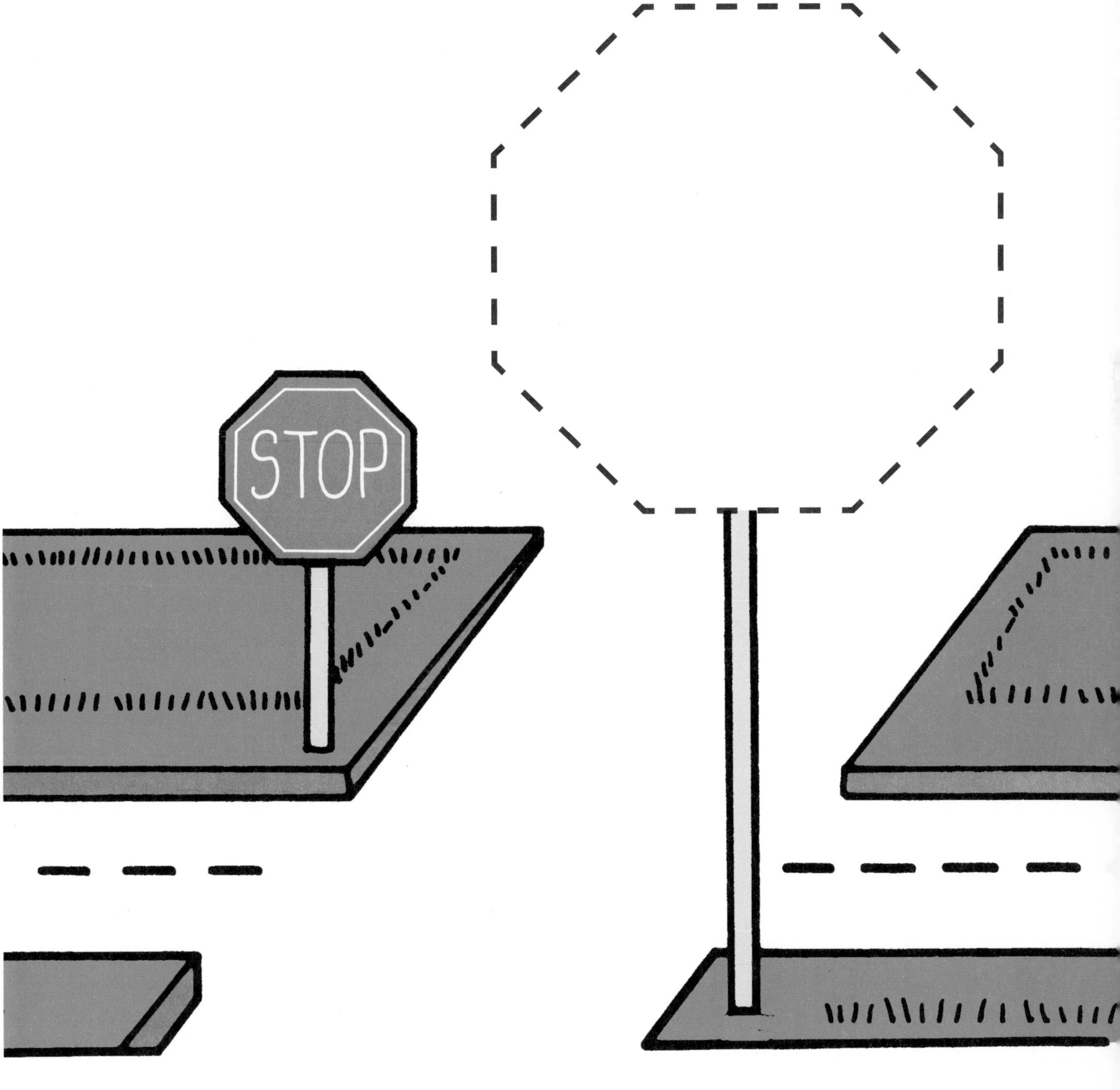

Color the picture. Use the color key.

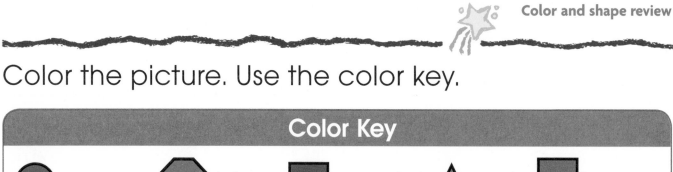

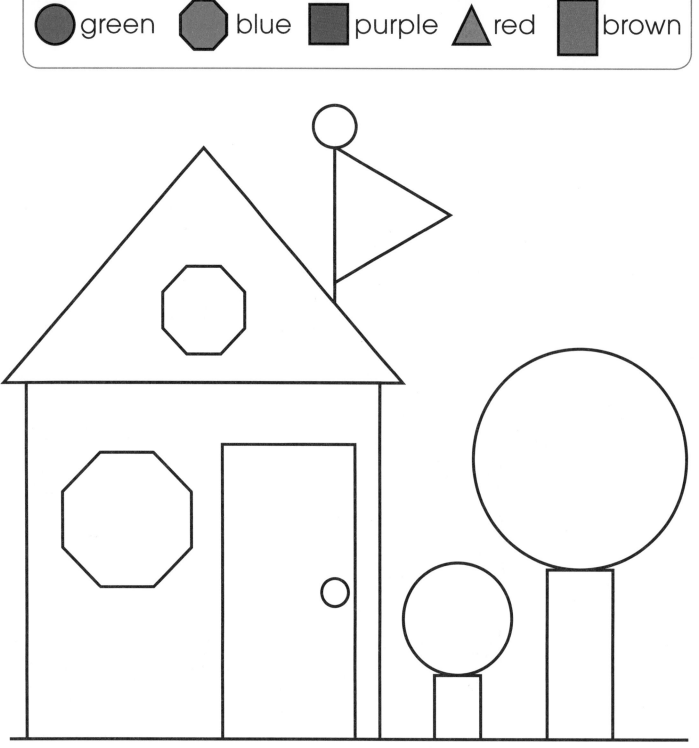

Color the picture. Use the color key.

Color Key

⬭ orange　⬡ red　⭐ yellow　◆ pink

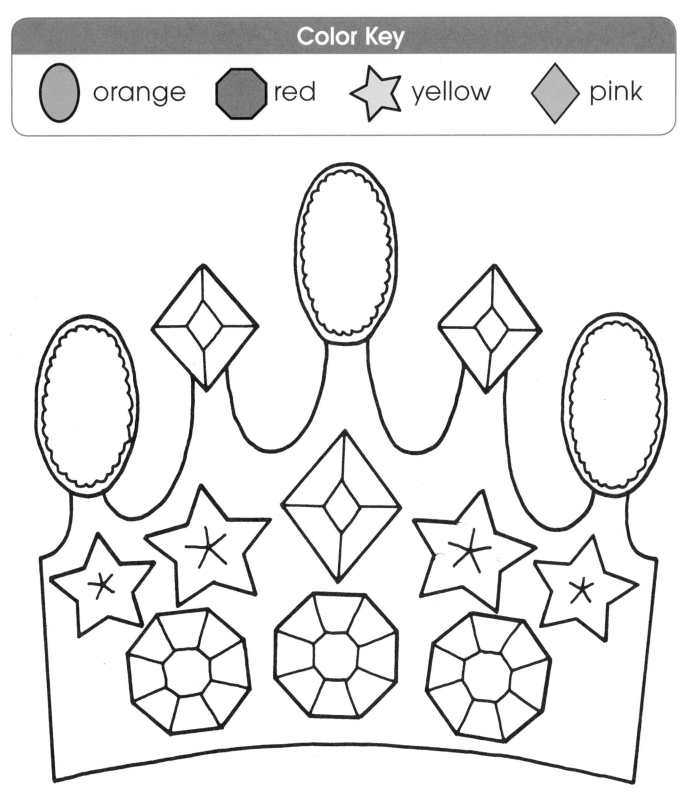

Draw a line to match the shape to its name.

 square

_____

- - - - - - - - - -

_____

▲ triangle

_____

- - - - - - - - - -

_____

 rectangle

_____

- - - - - - - - - -

_____

● circle

_____

- - - - - - - - - -

_____

Draw a line to match the shape to its name.

 oval

diamond

★ star

 octagon

Circle your favorite colors. Draw a picture using those colors.

COUNTING
AND PATTERNS

1

2

3

4

5

6

Count the animals in each set.
Write the number in the box.

Count the animals in each set.
Write the number in the box.

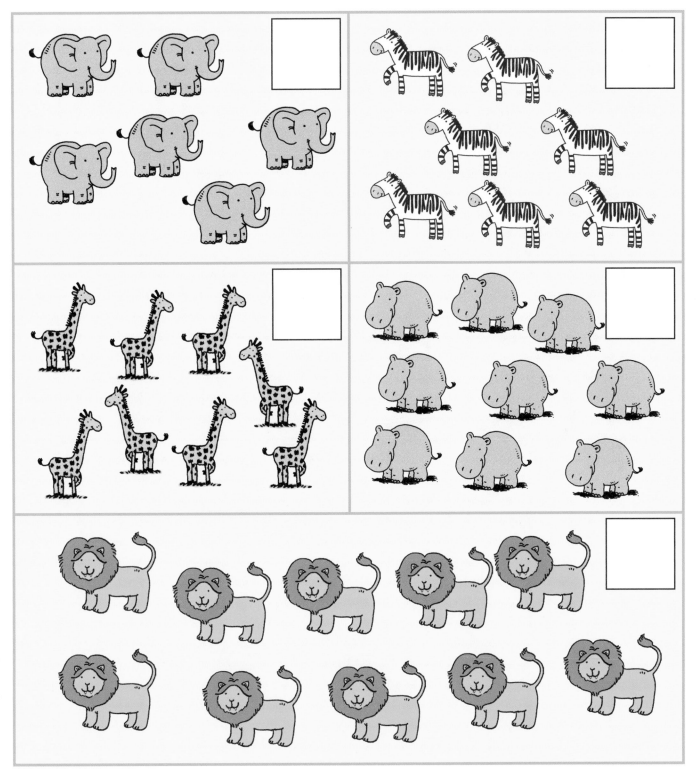

Count the fruit in the bowl.

I counted . . .

Count the flowers in the garden.

I counted . . .

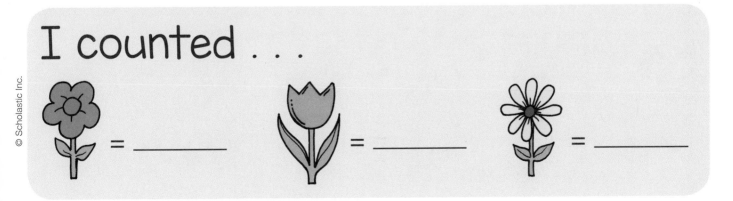

Count each item on the boy's face.

I counted . . . .

👁 = _____ 👃 = _____ 👂 = _____

〰 = _____ 👄 = _____ 🧢 = _____

Draw **1** spot on the fish.

Draw **2** spots on the fish.

Draw **3** spots on the fish.

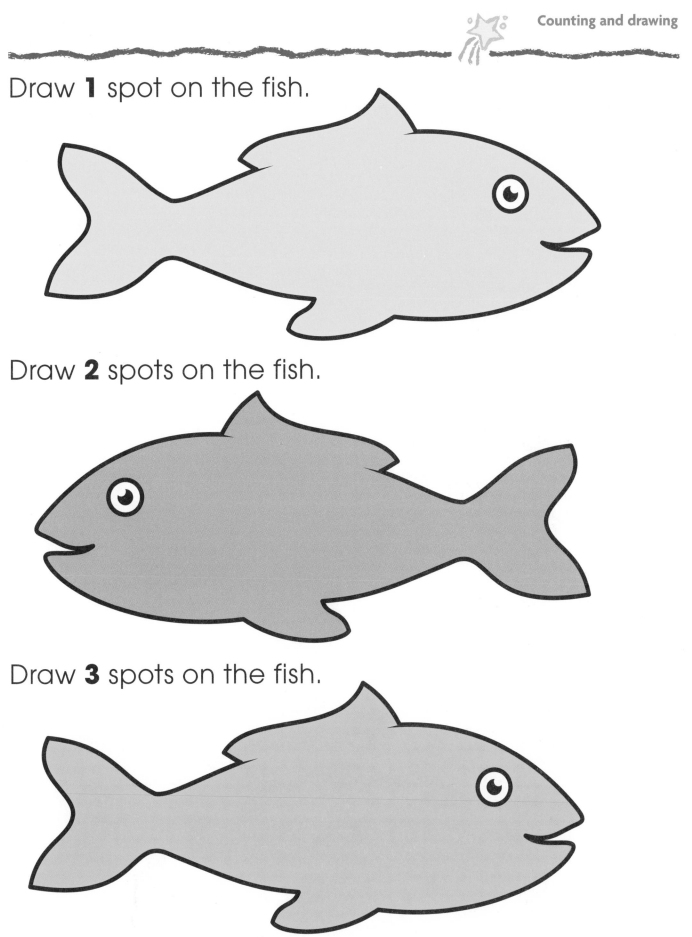

Draw **4** spots on the dog.

Draw **5** spots on the dog.

Draw **6** spots on the dog.

Draw **7** spots on the cat.

Draw **8** spots on the cat.

Draw **9** spots on the cat.

Draw **10** spots on the dinosaur.
Then give him a name.

My dinosaur's name is . . .

_____

- -

_____

Compare the sets in each pair of matching items. Circle the one that has **more**.

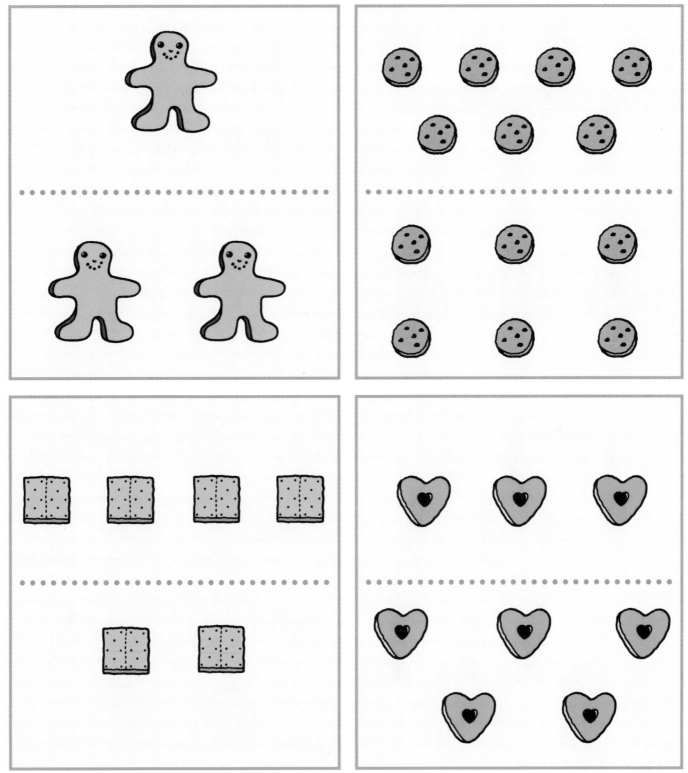

Compare the sets in each pair of matching items. Circle the one that has **more**.

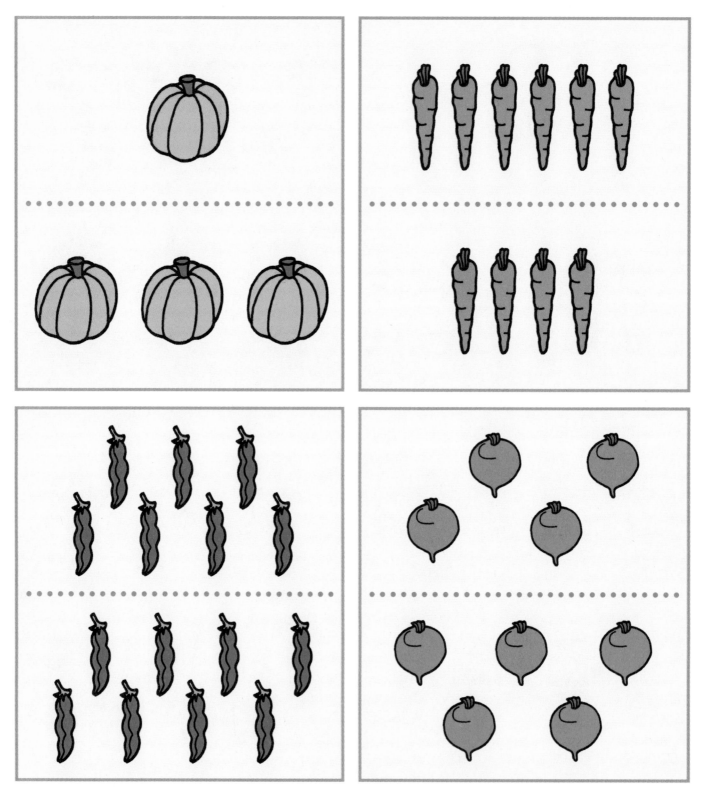

Compare the sets in each pair of matching items. Circle the one that has **fewer**.

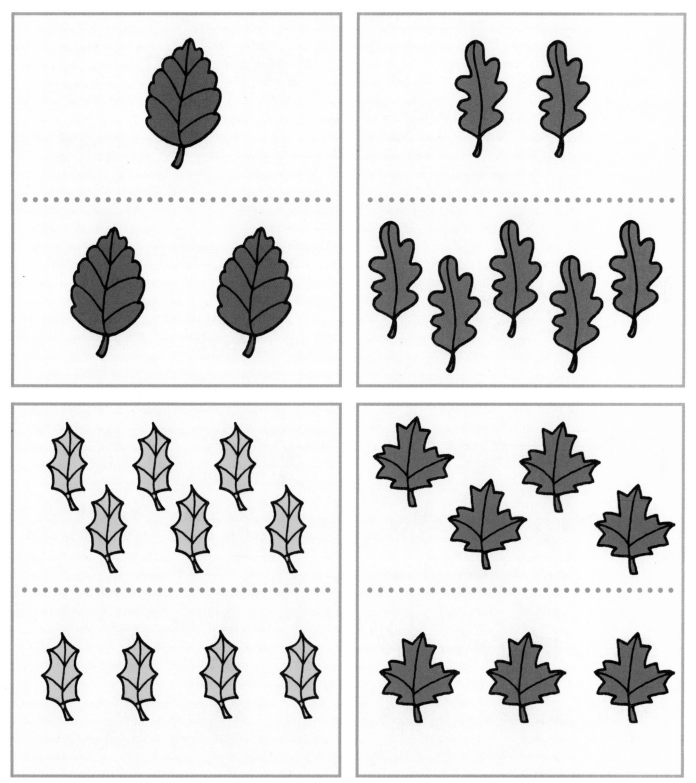

Compare the sets in each pair of matching items. Circle the one that has **fewer**.

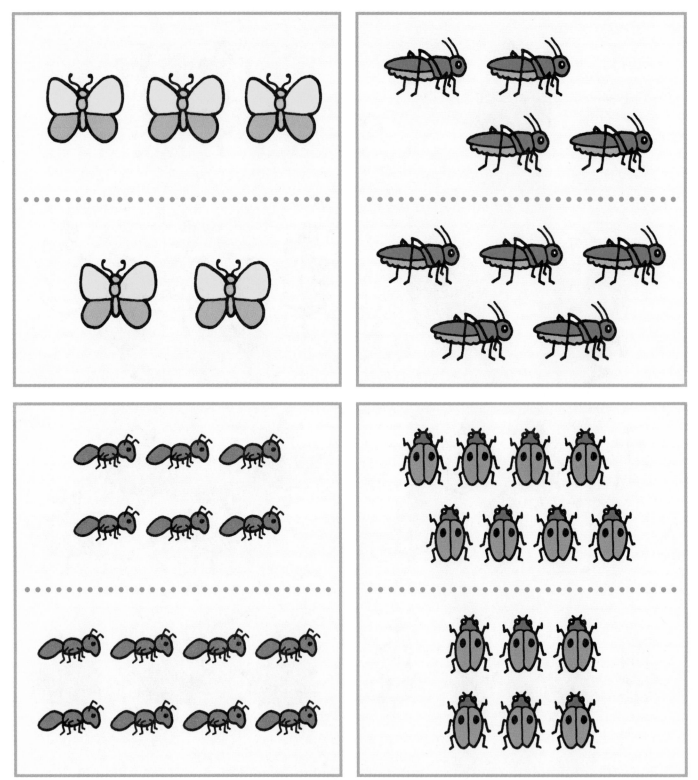

Draw a line from the number to its name.

three

one

five

two

four

Draw a line from the number to its name.

ten

seven

nine

six

eight

Write the missing numbers in each row.
Then circle the mouse that is not the same.

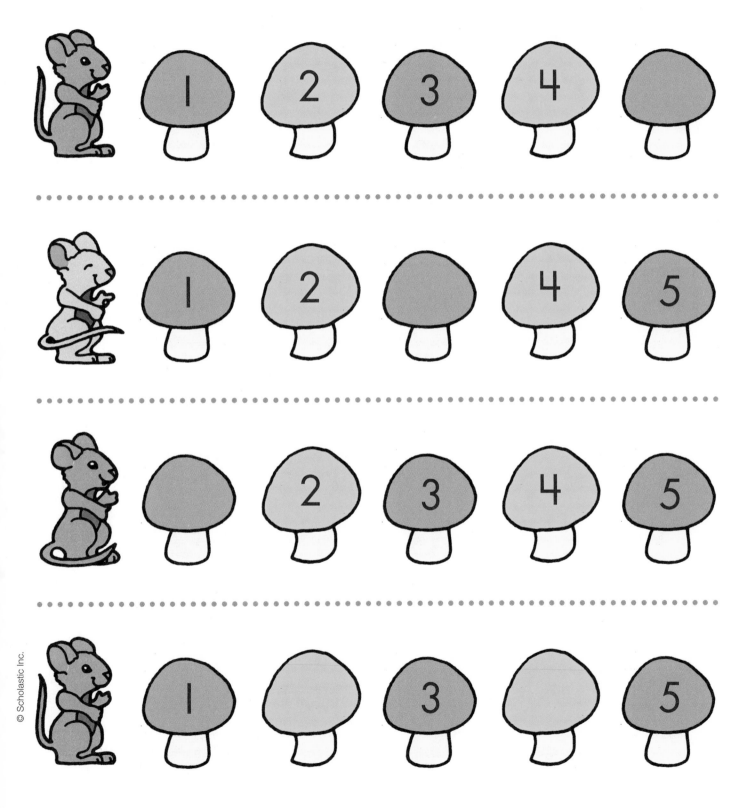

Write the missing numbers in each row.
Then circle the bee that is not the same.

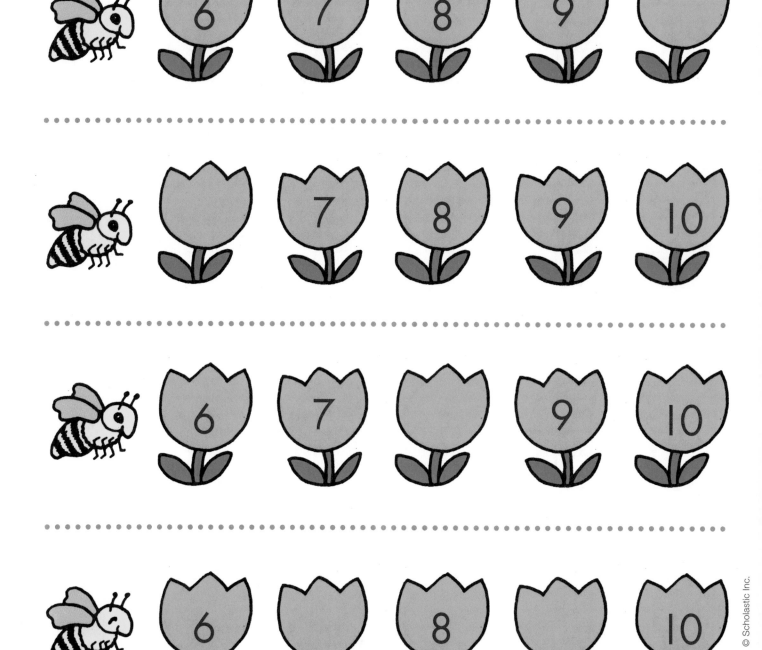

Count the leaves. Write the number of leaves in the tree. Then circle the caterpillar that is not the same.

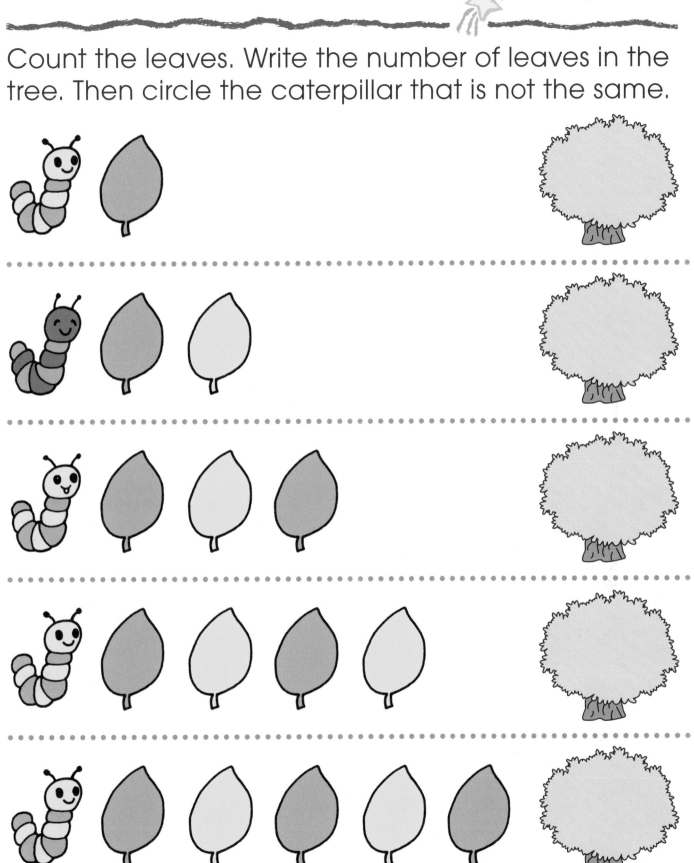

Count the eggs. Write the number of eggs in the nest. Then circle the chick that is not the same.

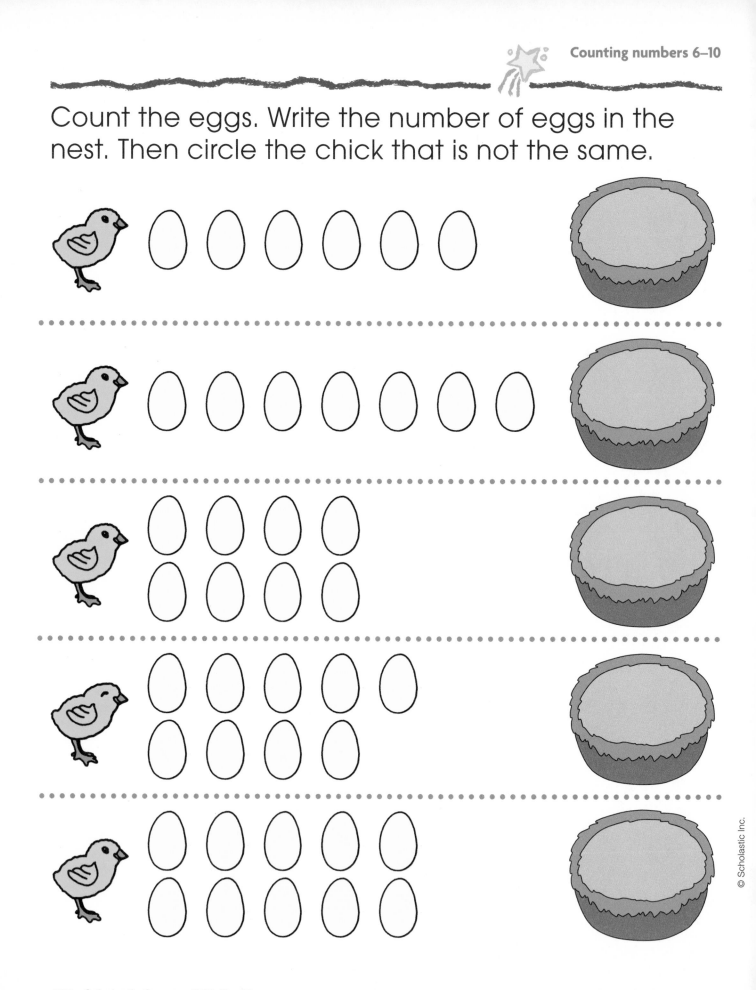

Count to 10 by filling in the missing numbers.

Count to 10 by filling in the missing numbers.

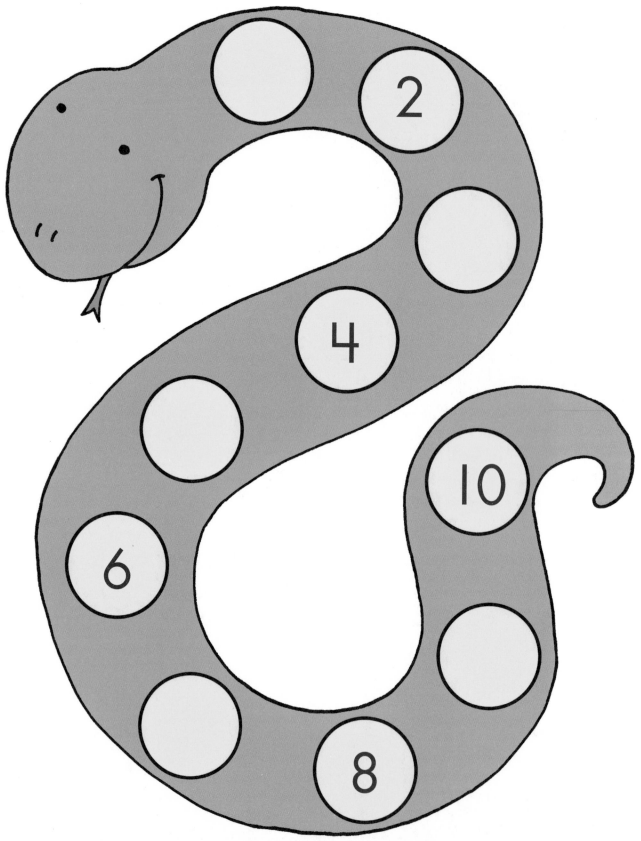

Use crayons and the key to make a color pattern.

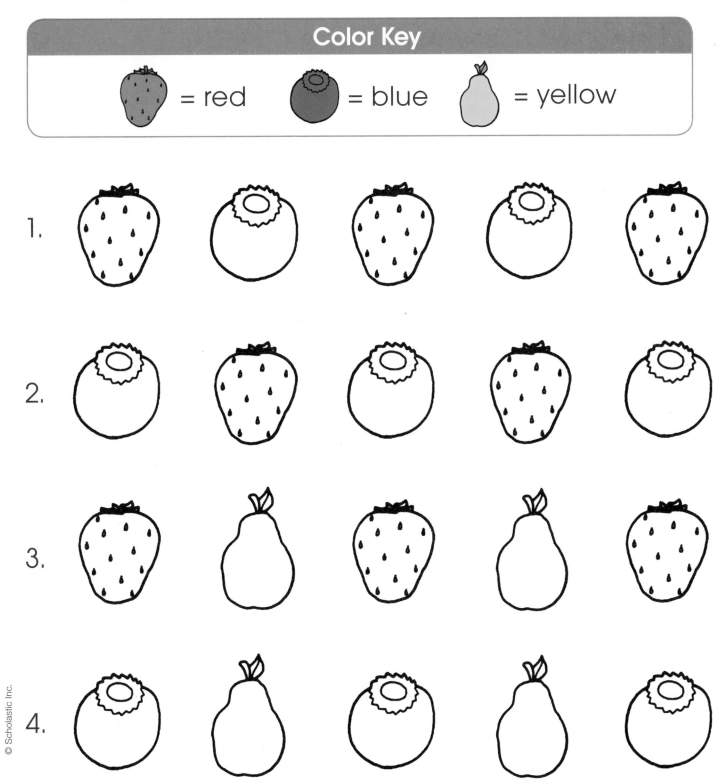

Use crayons and the key to make a color pattern.

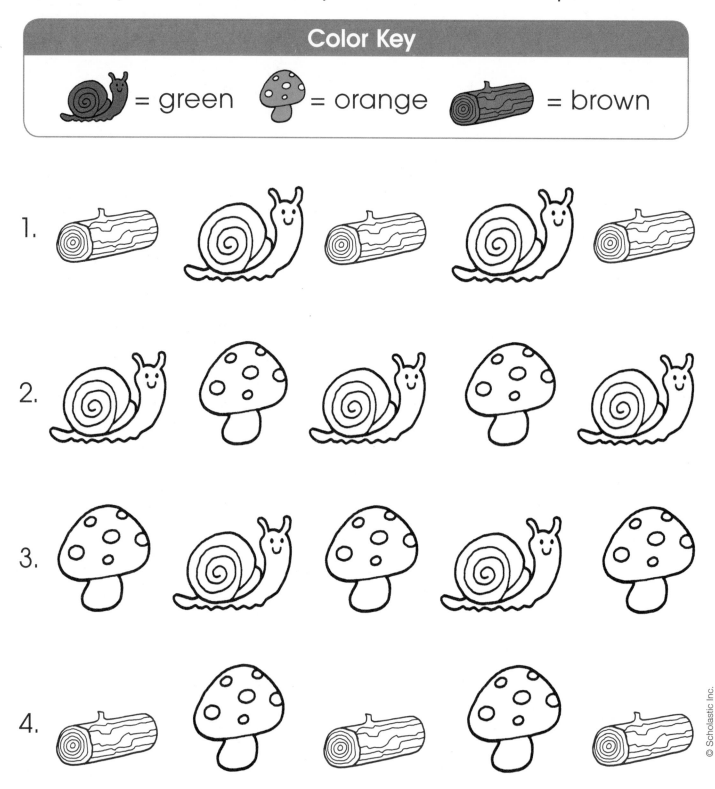

Color Key
= green = orange = brown

1.

2.

3.

4.

Use crayons and the key to make a color pattern.

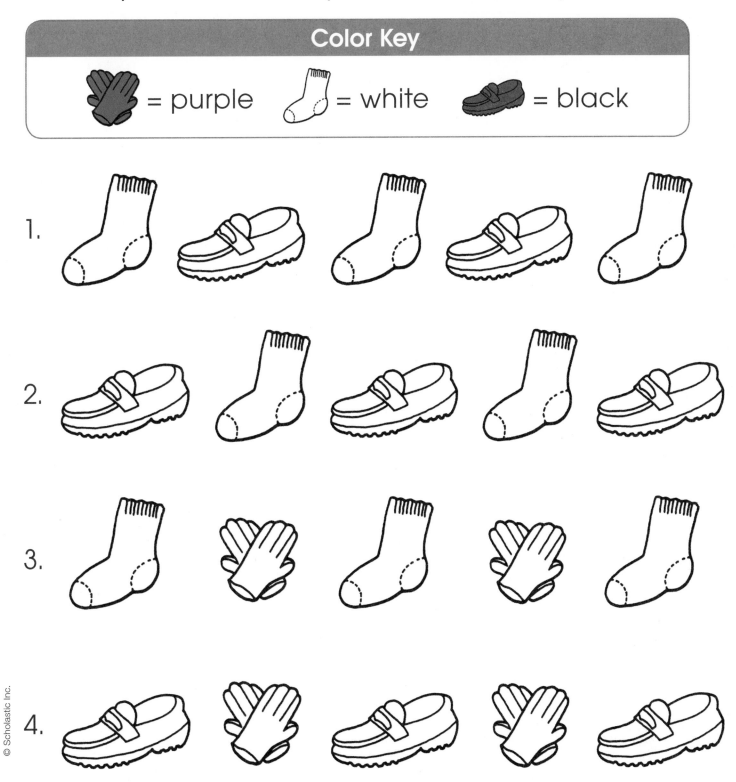

Use crayons and the key to make a color pattern

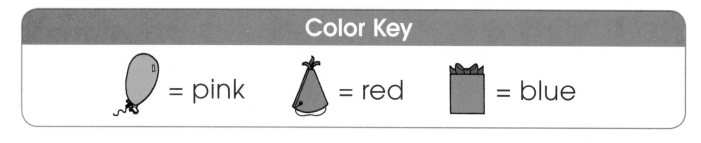

Color Key

= pink   = red   = blue

1.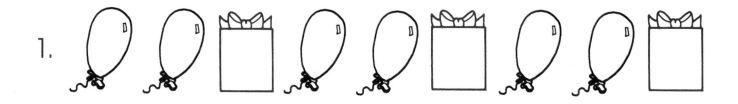

2.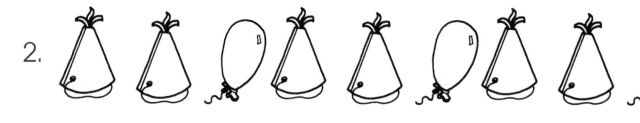

3.

4.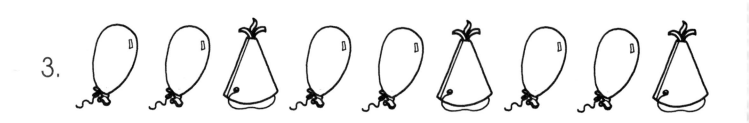

Draw and color the shape that comes next in each pattern.

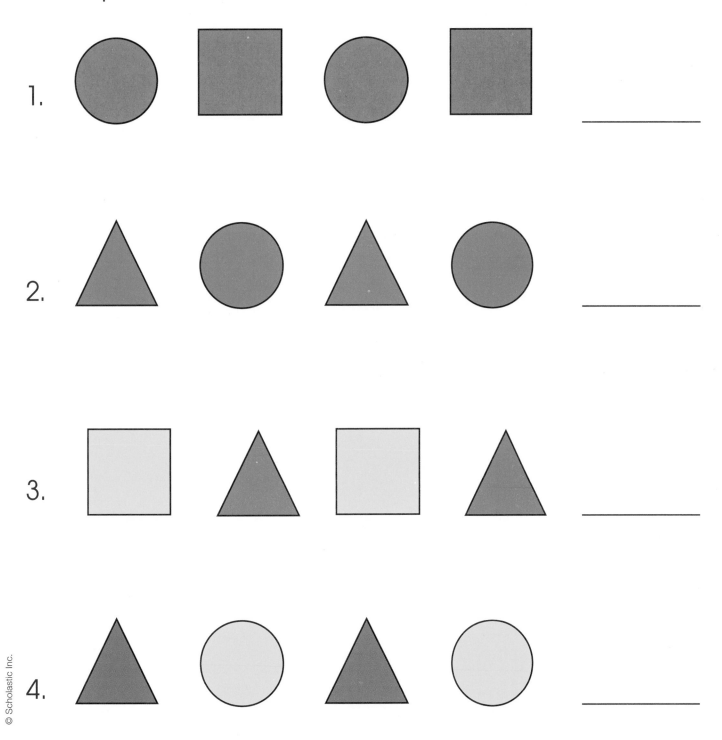

1.

2.

3.

4.

Draw and color the shape that comes next in each pattern.

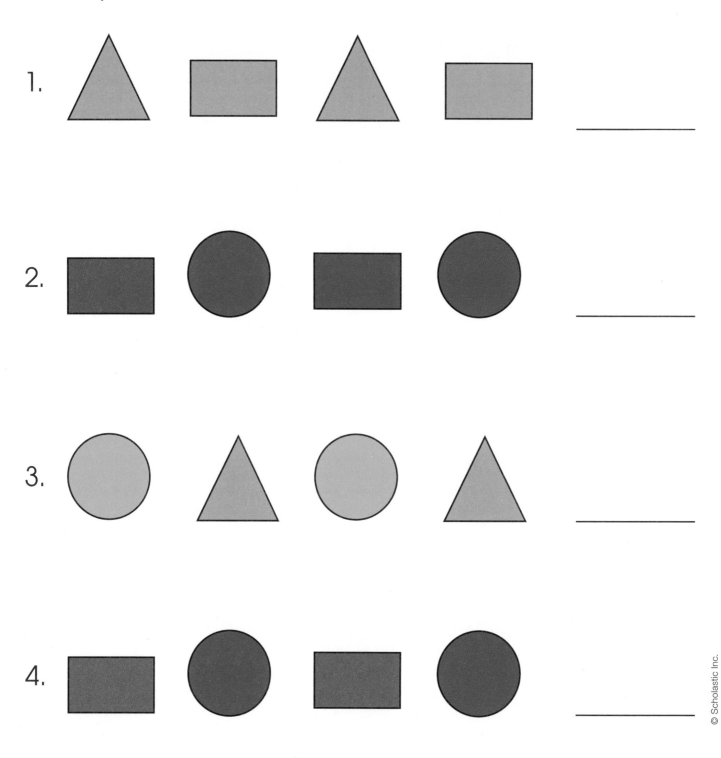

1.

2.

3.

4.

Draw and color the shape that comes next in each pattern.

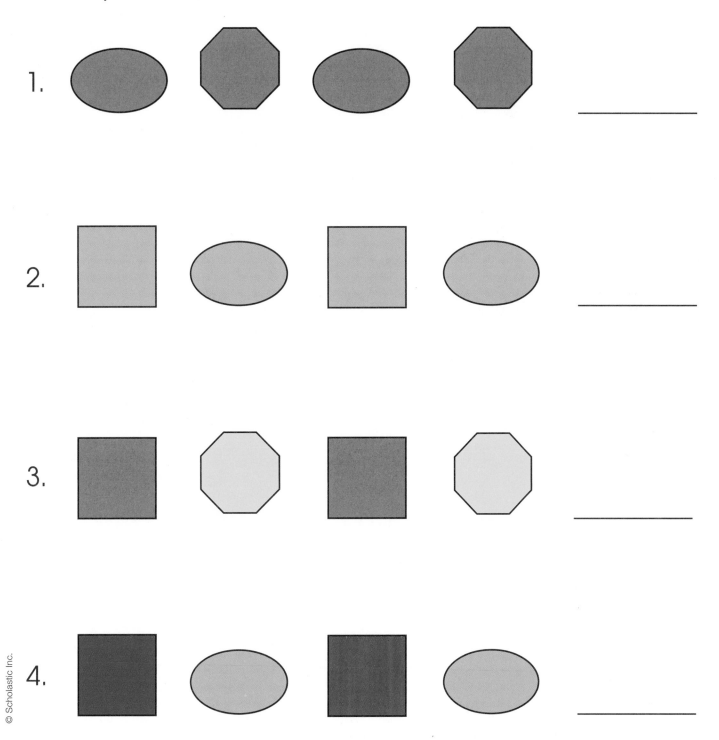

Draw and color the shape that comes next in each pattern.

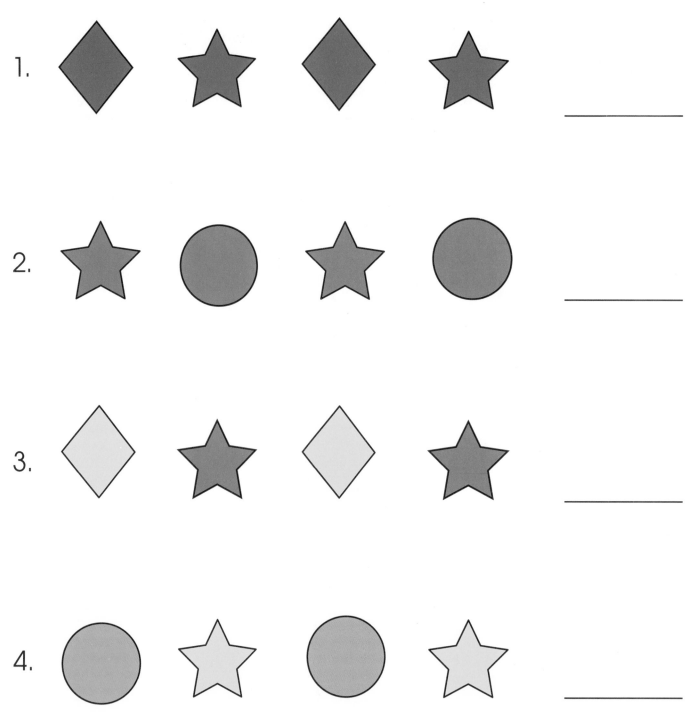

Use crayons to fill in the missing colored shapes on the T-shirt.

Use crayons to fill in the missing colored shapes on the T-shirt.

Use crayons to fill in the missing colored shapes on the T-shirt.

Draw colored shapes to make a pattern on the T-shirt. Then write your name at the bottom.

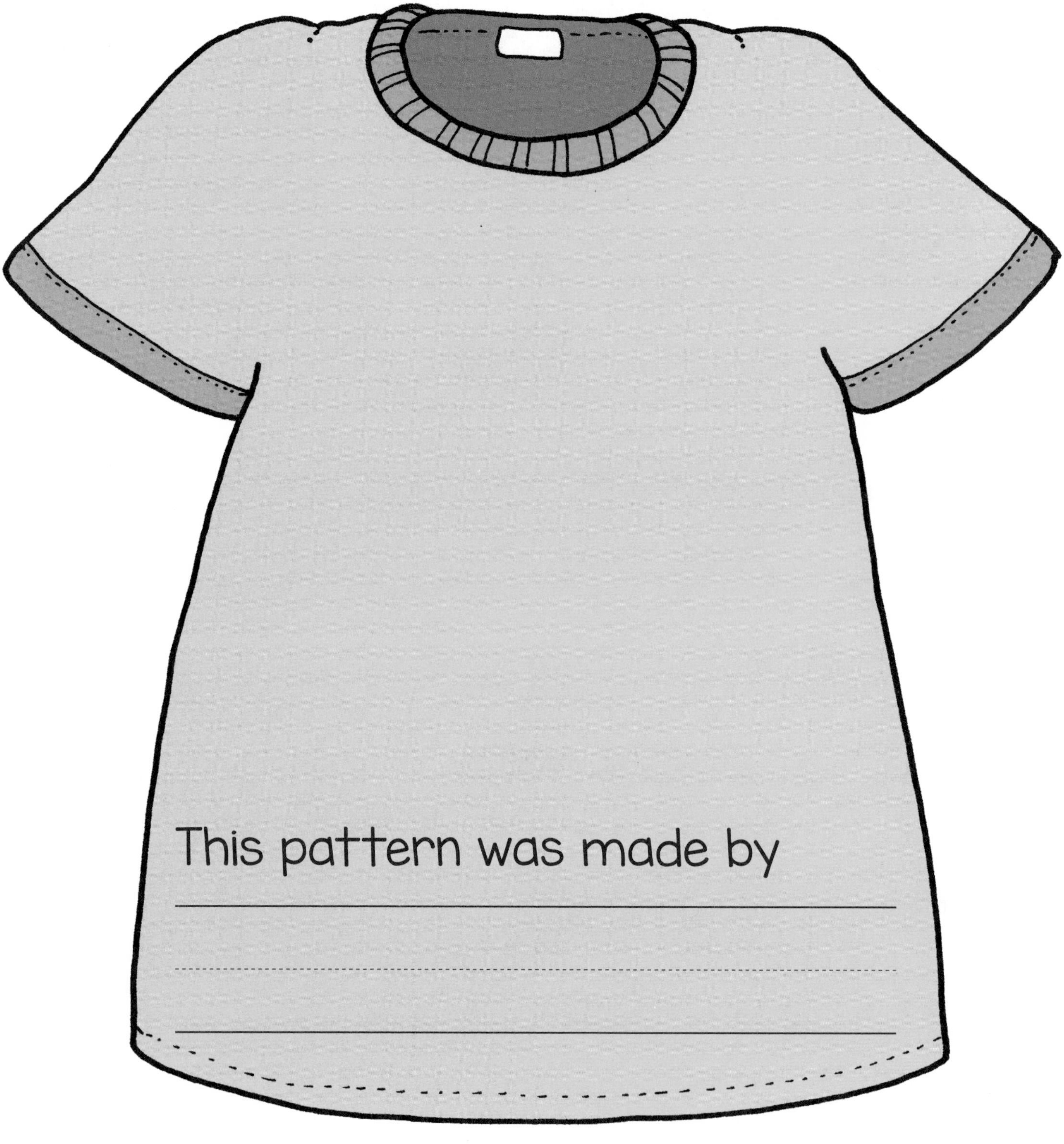

This pattern was made by

_____

- -

_____

Circle the animal that comes next in the pattern.

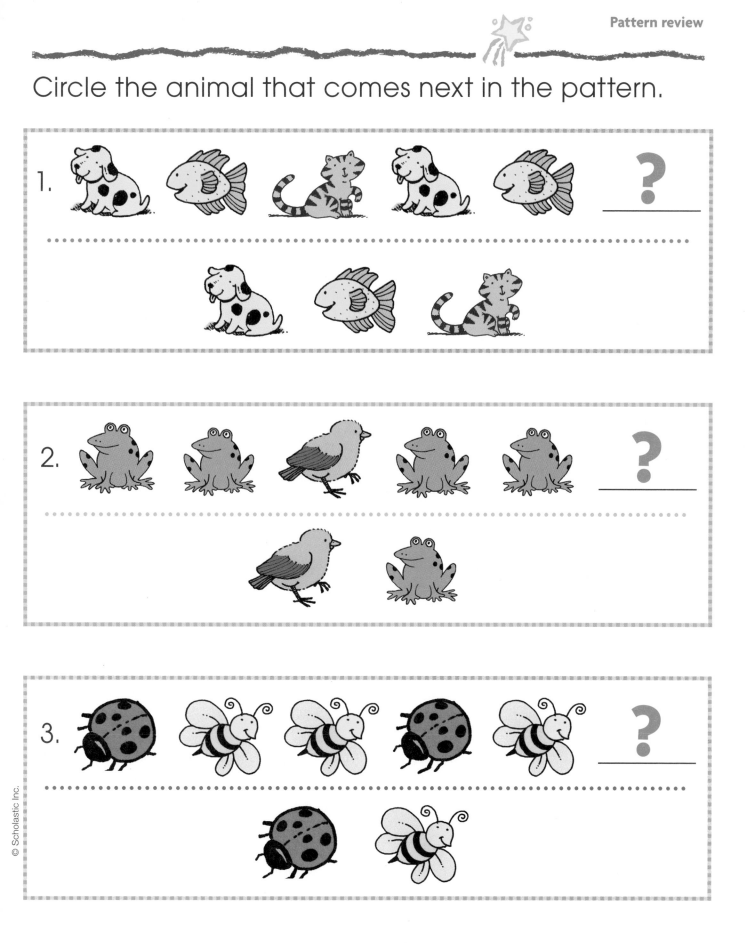

Circle the letter that comes next in the pattern.

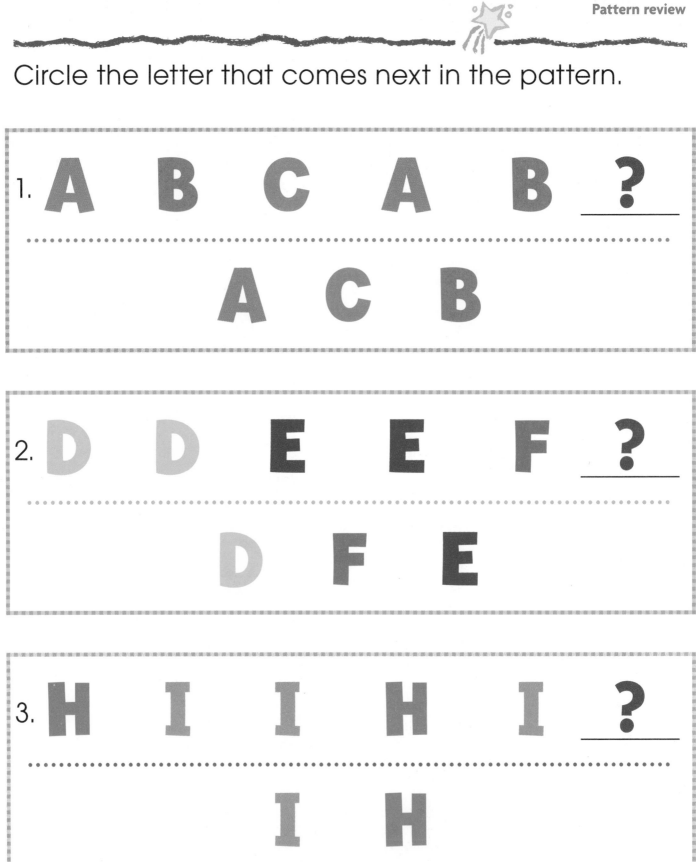

1. A B C A B ____?____

A C B

2. D D E E F ____?____

D F E

3. H I I H I ____?____

I H

PHONICS

Phonics Fun

This workbook section is here to help your child build a solid foundation in phonics by introducing initial letter sounds. In addition to the pages that follow, you can boost skills with one or all of these quick and fun activities.

1. **Letter List:** Select a letter and work with your child to brainstorm a long list of words that begin with that letter. Can you think of ten or more?

2. **Letter Clap:** Pick a letter. Then read a favorite story aloud, inviting your child to clap each time a word is read that begins with that letter.

3. **Letter Collage:** Use magazines and/or pictures downloaded from the Internet to craft a lively collage of items that begin with a specific letter.

4. **Edible Letter:** Encourage your child to build his or her favorite letter (or letters!) out of cereal, raisins, or pasta pieces.

5. **Letter Guess:** Select a letter and provide your child with a quick clue to its identity, such as: *It is the last letter of the alphabet and it begins the word "zoo."* Can your child guess it?

6. **Letter Hunt:** Challenge your child to look around the room and find as many items as possible that begin with a specific letter.

7. **Letter Match:** Write upper- and lowercase letters from A to Z on separate index cards. Then use them to play matching games.

8. **Letter Tongue Twister:** Make up a silly tongue twister that celebrates a specific letter such as: *Allie the alligator absolutely adores awesome apples!* Can your child say it five times fast?

Name each picture. Draw a line from the alligator to each picture that begins with the letter **a**.

Write the beginning letter for each picture.

_____   _____   _____   _____

_____   _____   _____   _____

Name each picture. Draw a line from the bat to each picture that begins with the letter **b**.

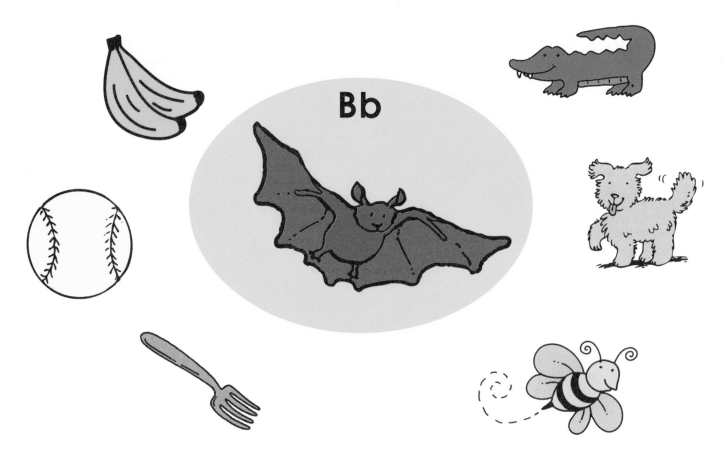

Write the beginning letter for each picture.

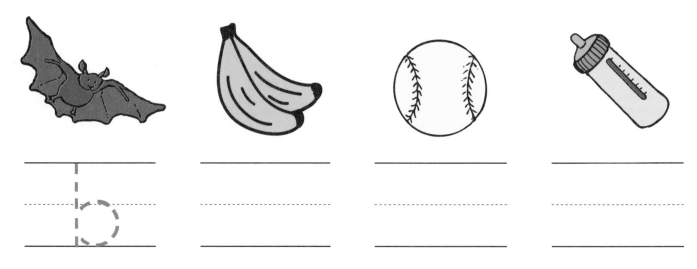

Name each picture. Draw a line from the cat to each picture that begins with the letter **c**.

Write the beginning letter for each picture.

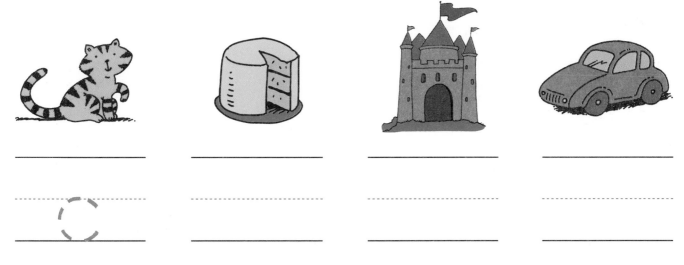

Name each picture. Draw a line from the dog to each picture that begins with the letter **d**.

Write the beginning letter for each picture.

Name each picture. Draw a line from the elephant to each picture that begins with the letter **e**.

Write the beginning letter for each picture.

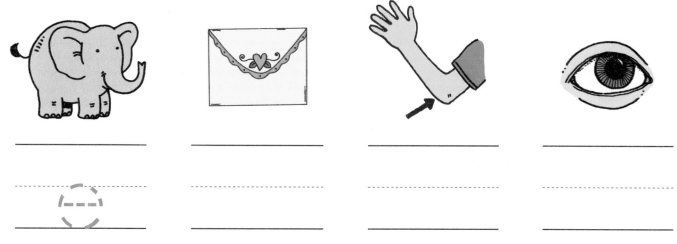

© Scholastic Inc.

Name each picture. Draw a line from the fish to each picture that begins with the letter **f**.

Write the beginning letter for each picture.

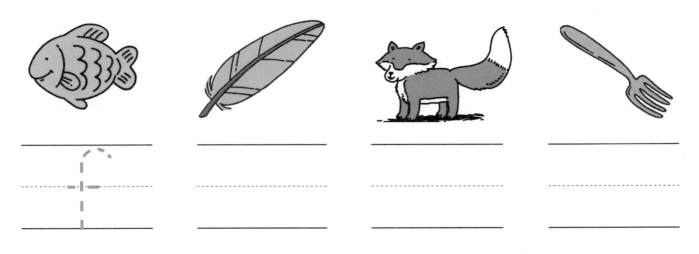

Name each picture. Draw a line from the goat to each picture that begins with the letter **g**.

Write the beginning letter for each picture.

Name each picture. Draw a line from the horse to each picture that begins with the letter **h**.

Write the beginning letter for each picture.

Name each picture. Draw a line from the iguana to each picture that begins with the letter **i**.

Write the beginning letter for each picture.

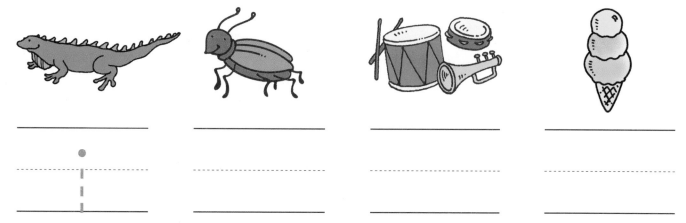

Name each picture. Draw a line from the jellyfish to each picture that begins with the letter **j**.

Write the beginning letter for each picture.

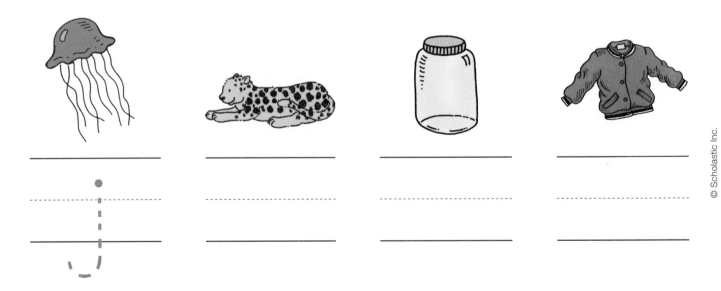

Name each picture. Draw a line from the kangaroo to each picture that begins with the letter **k**.

Write the beginning letter for each picture.

Name each picture. Draw a line from the lion to each picture that begins with the letter **l**.

Write the beginning letter for each picture.

Name each picture. Draw a line from the mouse to each picture that begins with the letter **m**.

Write the beginning letter for each picture.

Name each picture. Draw a line from the newt to each picture that begins with the letter **n**.

Write the beginning letter for each picture.

Name each picture. Draw a line from the ostrich to each picture that begins with the letter **o**.

Write the beginning letter for each picture.

Name each picture. Draw a line from the pig to each picture that begins with the letter **p**.

Write the beginning letter for each picture.

Name each picture. Draw a line from the queen to each picture that begins with the letter **q**.

Write the beginning letter for each picture.

Name each picture. Draw a line from the racoon to each picture that begins with the letter **r**.

Write the beginning letter for each picture.

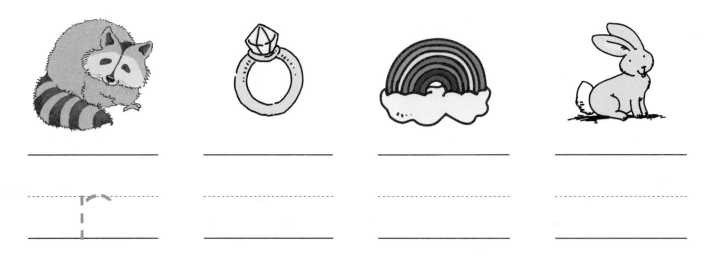

Name each picture. Draw a line from the seal to each picture that begins with the letter **s**.

Write the beginning letter for each picture.

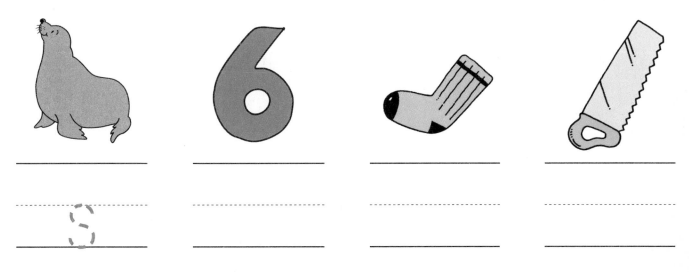

Name each picture. Draw a line from the turtle to each picture that begins with the letter **t**.

Write the beginning letter for each picture.

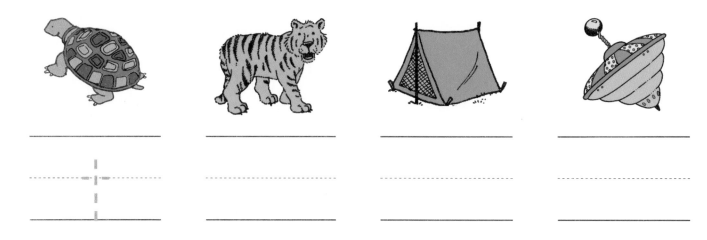

Name each picture. Draw a line from the umbrella to each picture that begins with the letter **u**.

Write the beginning letter for each picture.

Name each picture. Draw a line from the van to each picture that begins with the letter **v**.

Write the beginning letter for each picture.

Name each picture. Draw a line from the walrus to each picture that begins with the letter **w**.

Write the beginning letter for each picture.

Name each picture. Draw a line from the x-ray to each picture that begins with the letter **x**.

Write the beginning letter for each picture.

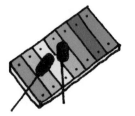

_____ _____

- - - - X - - - -   - - - - - - - - -

_____ _____

Name each picture. Draw a line from the yak to each picture that begins with the letter **y**.

Write the beginning letter for each picture.

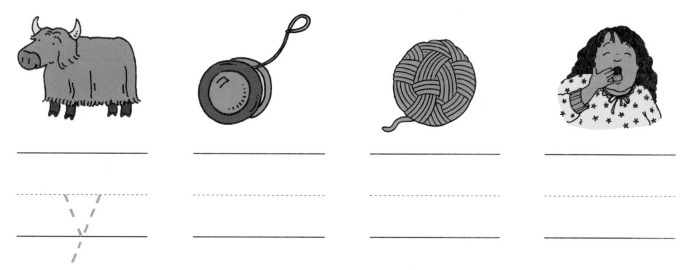

© Scholastic Inc.

Name each picture. Draw a line from the zebra to each picture that begins with the letter **z**.

Write the beginning letter for each picture.

Name each picture. Circle the letter it begins with.

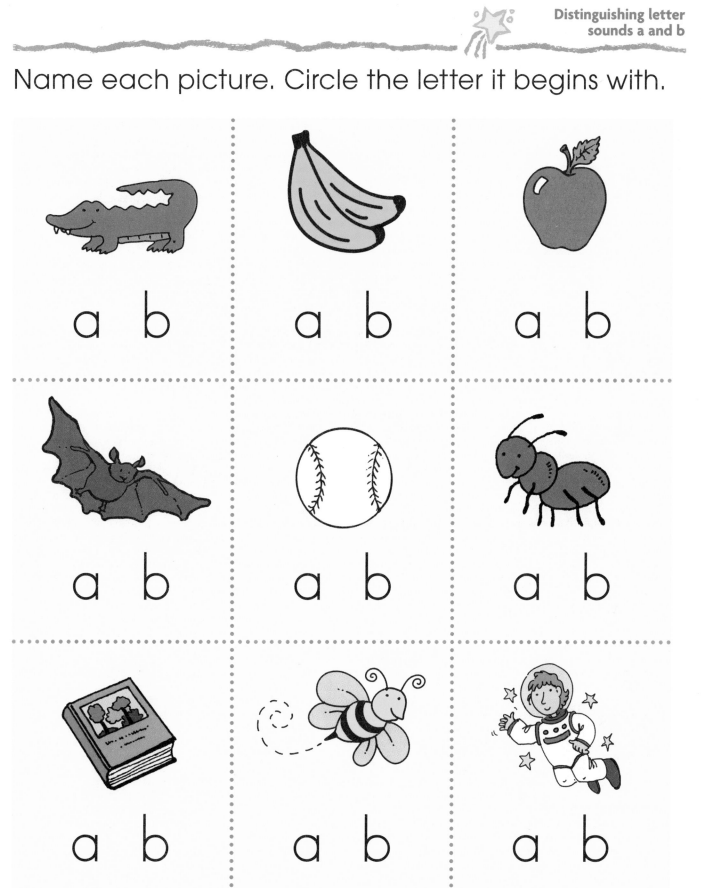

a b

a b

a b

a b

a b

a b

a b

a b

a b

Name each picture. Circle the letter it begins with.

c   d   c   d   c   d

c   d   c   d   c   d

c   d   c   d   c   d

Name each picture. Circle the letter it begins with.

e   f   e   f   e   f

e   f   e   f   e   f

e   f   e   f   e   f

Name each picture. Circle the letter it begins with.

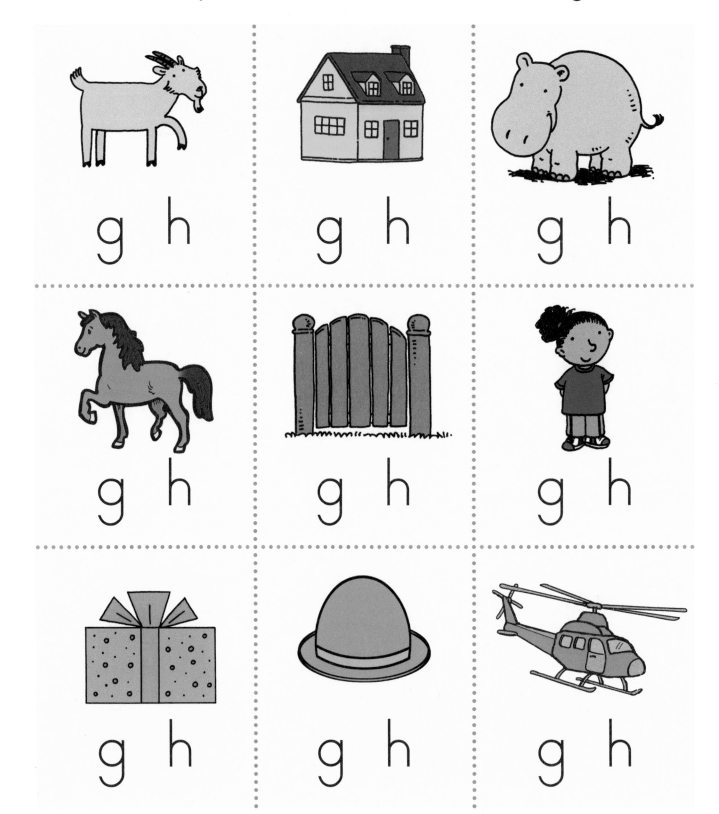

g h

g h

g h

g h

g h

g h

g h

g h

g h

Name each picture. Circle the letter it begins with.

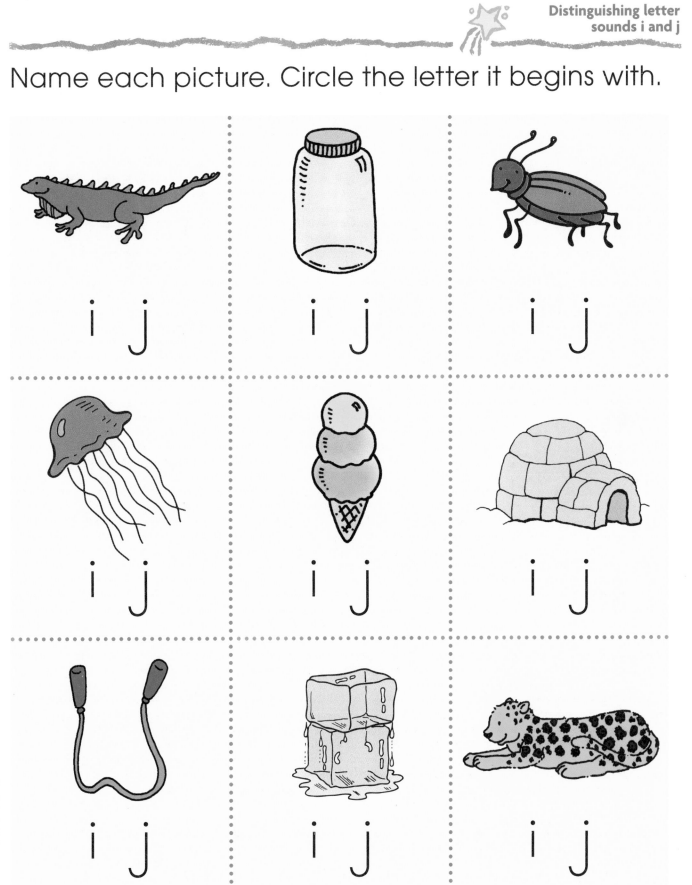

i j

i j

i j

i j

i j

i j

i j

i j

i j

Name each picture. Circle the letter it begins with.

k l   k l   k l

k l   k l   k l

k l   k l   k l

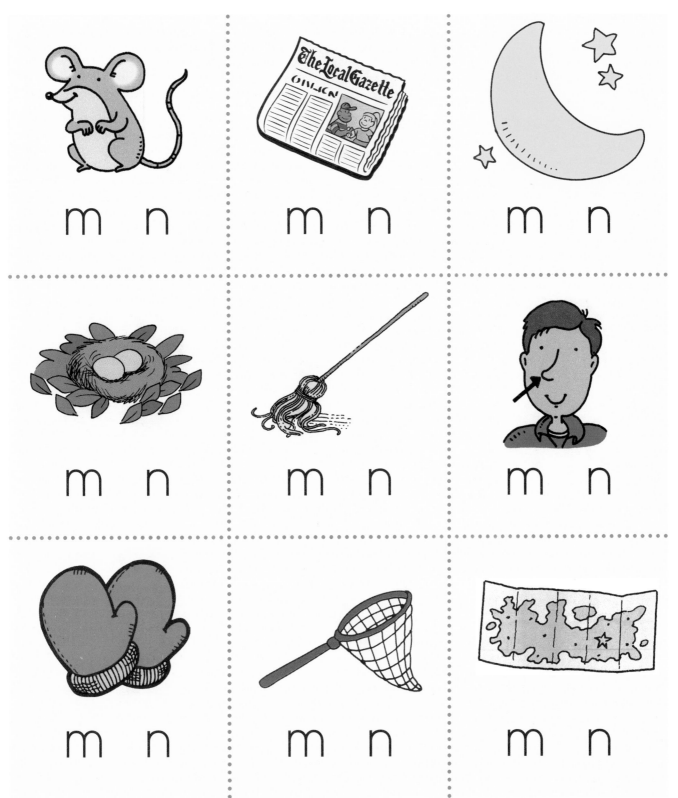

Name each picture. Circle the letter it begins with.

m   n   m   n   m   n

m   n   m   n   m   n

m   n   m   n   m   n

Name each picture. Circle the letter it begins with.

Name each picture. Circle the letter it begins with.

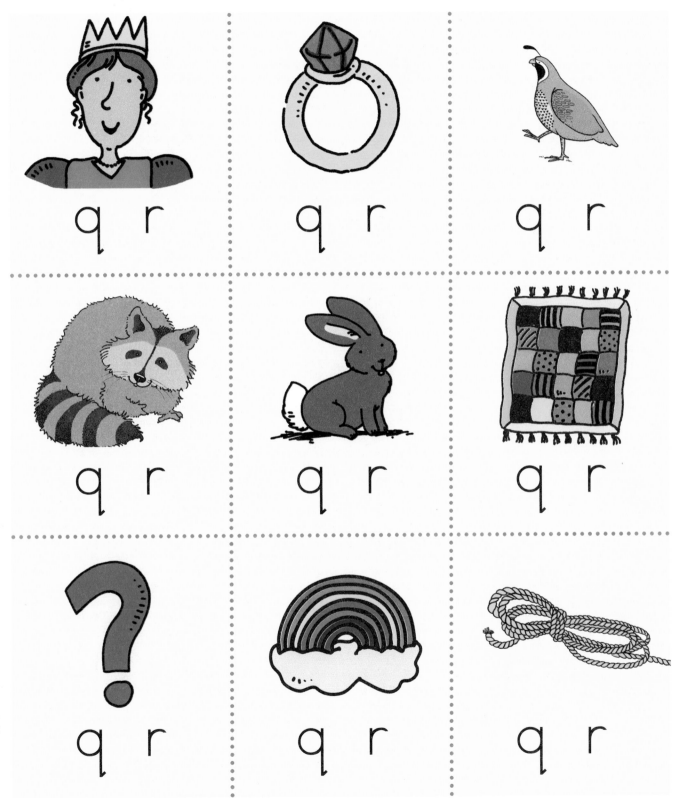

q r · q r · q r

q r · q r · q r

q r · q r · q r

Name each picture. Circle the letter it begins with.

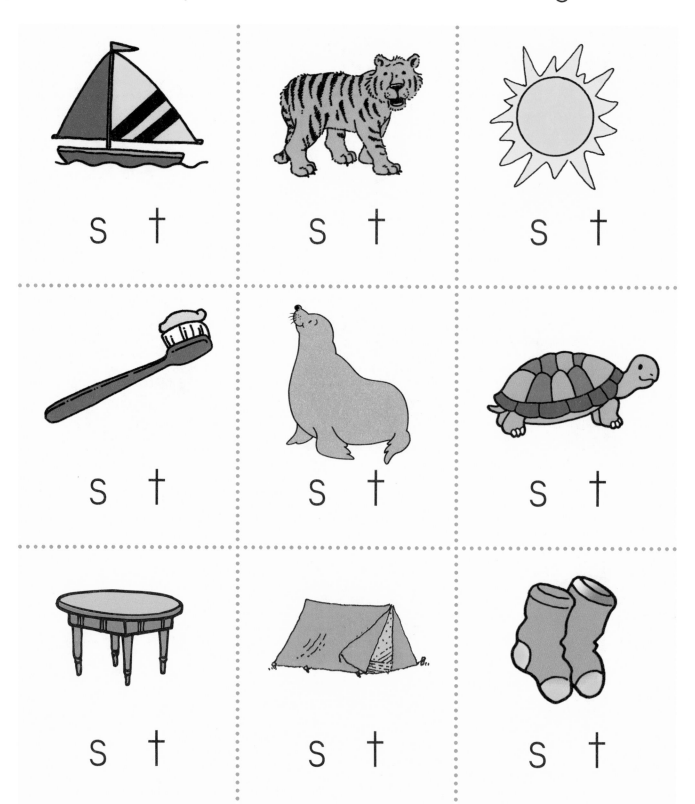

s t   s t   s t

s t   s t   s t

s t   s t   s t

Name each picture. Circle the letter it begins with.

u   v   u   v   u   v

u   v   u   v   u   v

u   v   u   v   u   v

Name each picture. Circle the letter it begins with.

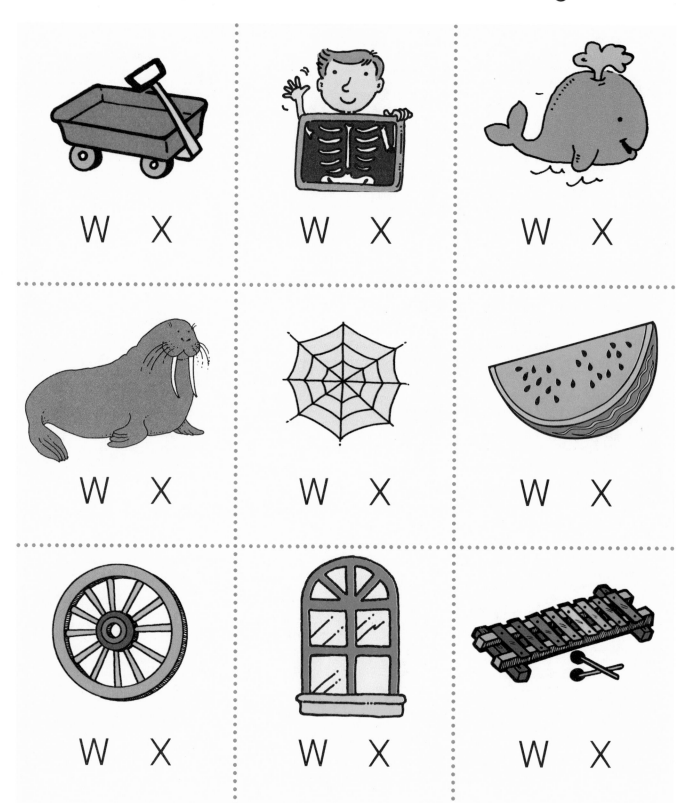

W X   W X   W X

W X   W X   W X

W X   W X   W X

Name each picture. Circle the letter it begins with.

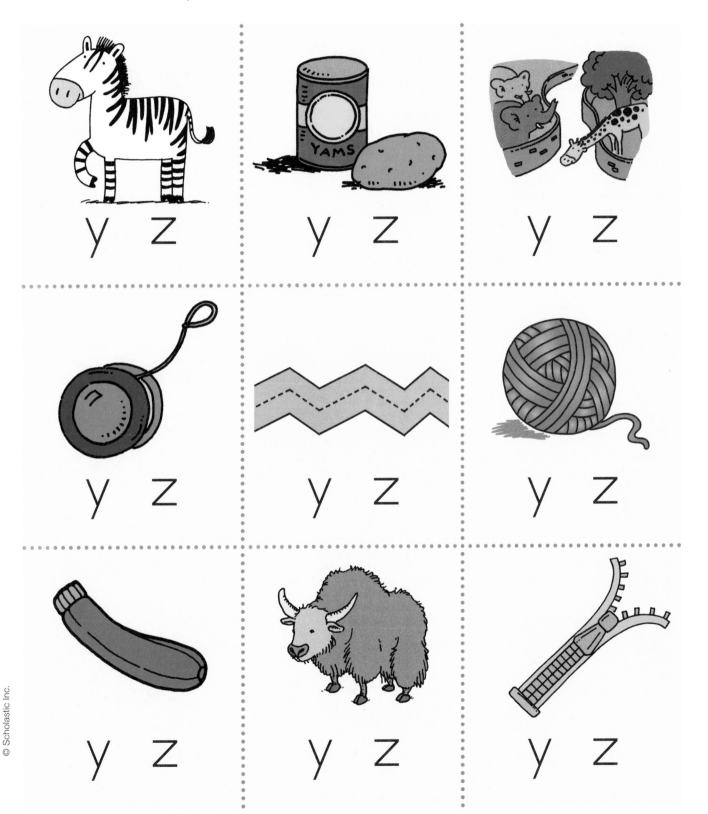

Look at the pictures. Fill in the missing letters.

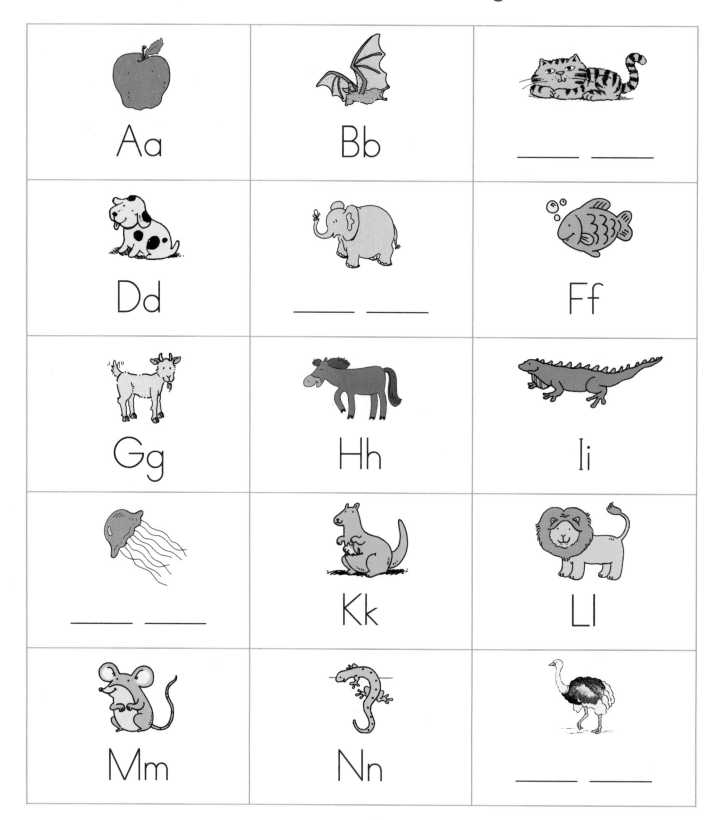

Aa

Bb

____ ____

Dd

____ ____

Ff

Gg

Hh

Ii

____ ____

Kk

Ll

Mm

Nn

____ ____

Look at the pictures. Fill in the missing letters.

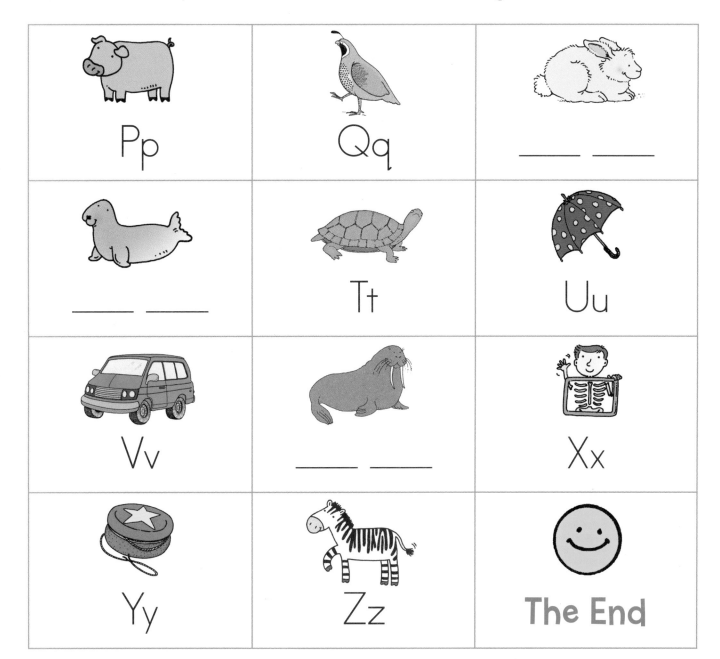

Pp

Qq

___ ___

___ ___

Tt

Uu

Vv

___ ___

Xx

Yy

Zz

The End

My favorite letter is _____

because _____.

Say your name. Write it on the line.

Circle the **first** letter in your name.

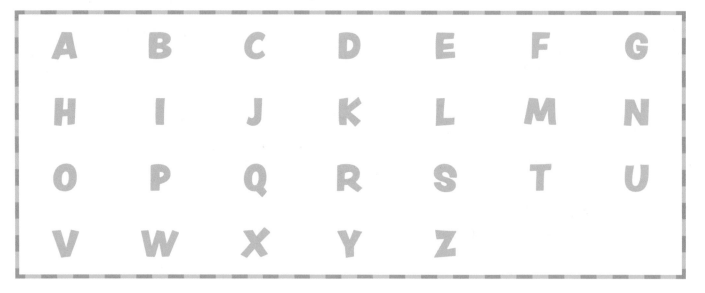

A	B	C	D	E	F	G
H	I	J	K	L	M	N
O	P	Q	R	S	T	U
V	W	X	Y	Z		

Circle the **last** letter in your name.

A	B	C	D	E	F	G
H	I	J	K	L	M	N
O	P	Q	R	S	T	U
V	W	X	Y	Z		

MY FIRST ALPHABET BOOKS

How to assemble My First Alphabet Books:

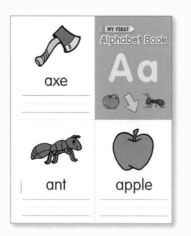

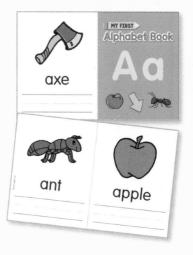

1. Tear out the page along the perforation.

2. Cut the page apart along the dashed line.

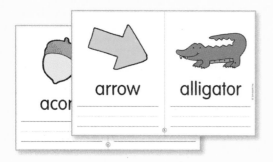

3. Place spread B on top of spread A, as shown, to make one book.

4. Staple the book along the spine. Then fold the pages along the solid lines.

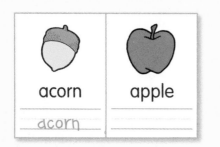

5. Invite your child to rewrite each alphabet word on the line.

6. Read the books together to boost phonemic awareness and literacy confidence. There is no such thing as reading a book too many times!

axe

- - - - - - - - - - - - - - - - - -

Alphabet Book

Aa

ant

- - - - - - - - - - - - - - - - - -

apple

- - - - - - - - - - - - - - - - - -

acorn

airplane

(A)

arrow

alligator

(B)

bear

Alphabet Book

B b

book

ball

bird

bike

bee

balloons

cupcake

MY FIRST

Alphabet Book

C c

cat

cup

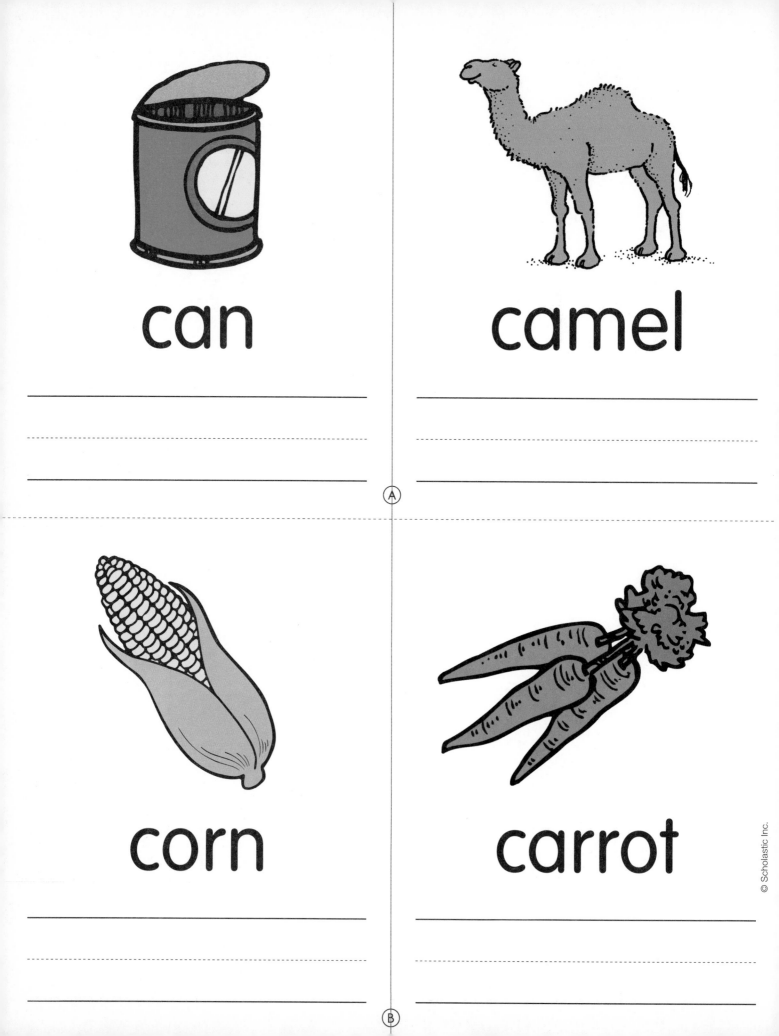

can

camel

corn

carrot

dolphin

Alphabet Book

Dd

dog

duck

dino

dice

doll

deer

elephant

Ee

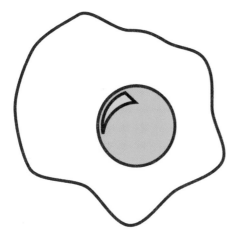

egg

elf

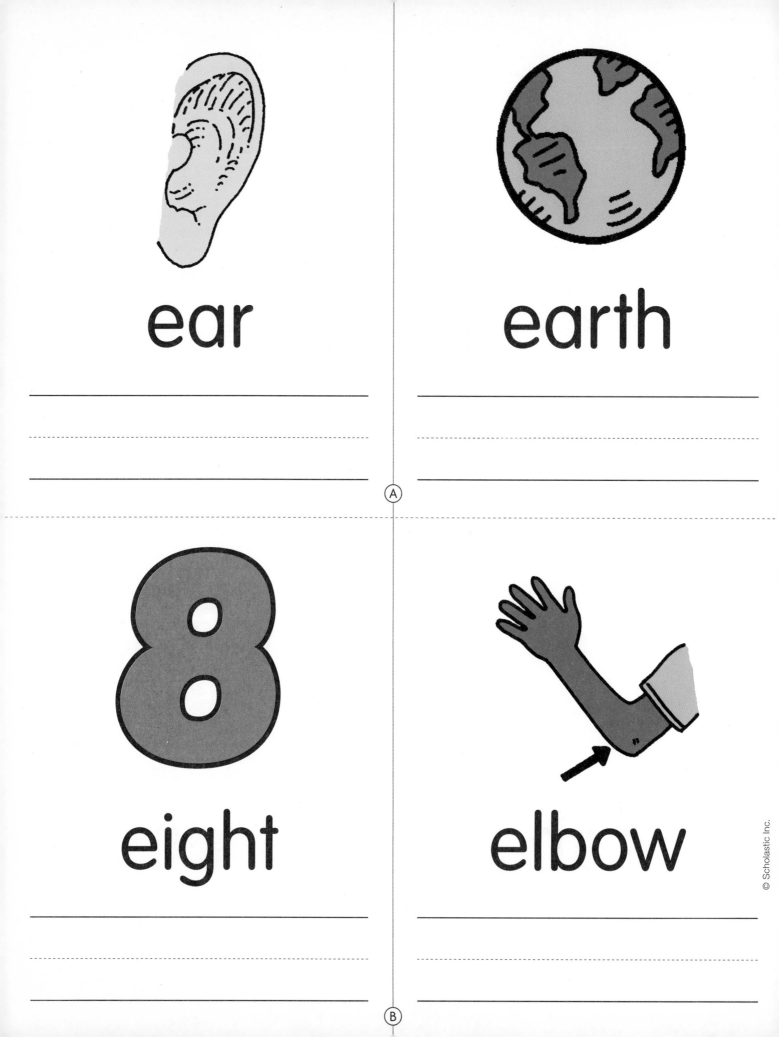

ear

earth

(A)

eight

elbow

(B)

© Scholastic Inc.

feather

_____

- - - - - - - - - - -

_____

F f

fish

_____

- - - - - - - - - - -

fan

_____

- - - - - - - - - - -

fire

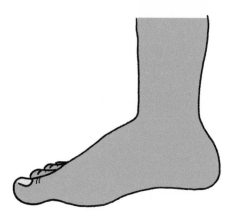

foot

(A)

football

fox

(B)

gopher

girl

gift

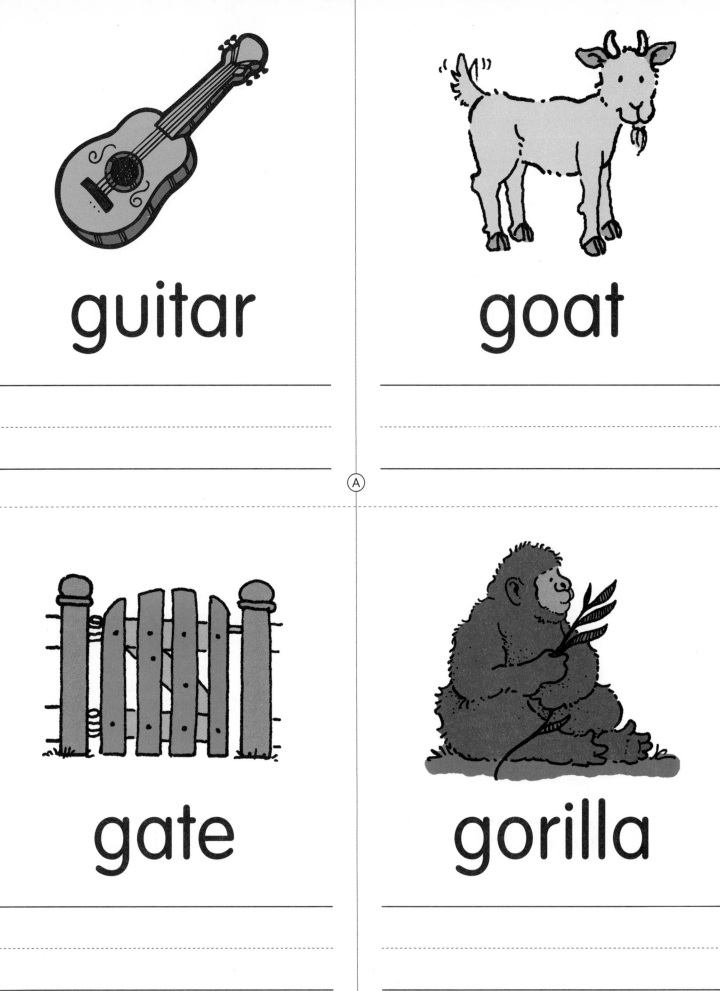

guitar

goat

gate

gorilla

hamster

hose

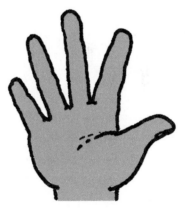

hand

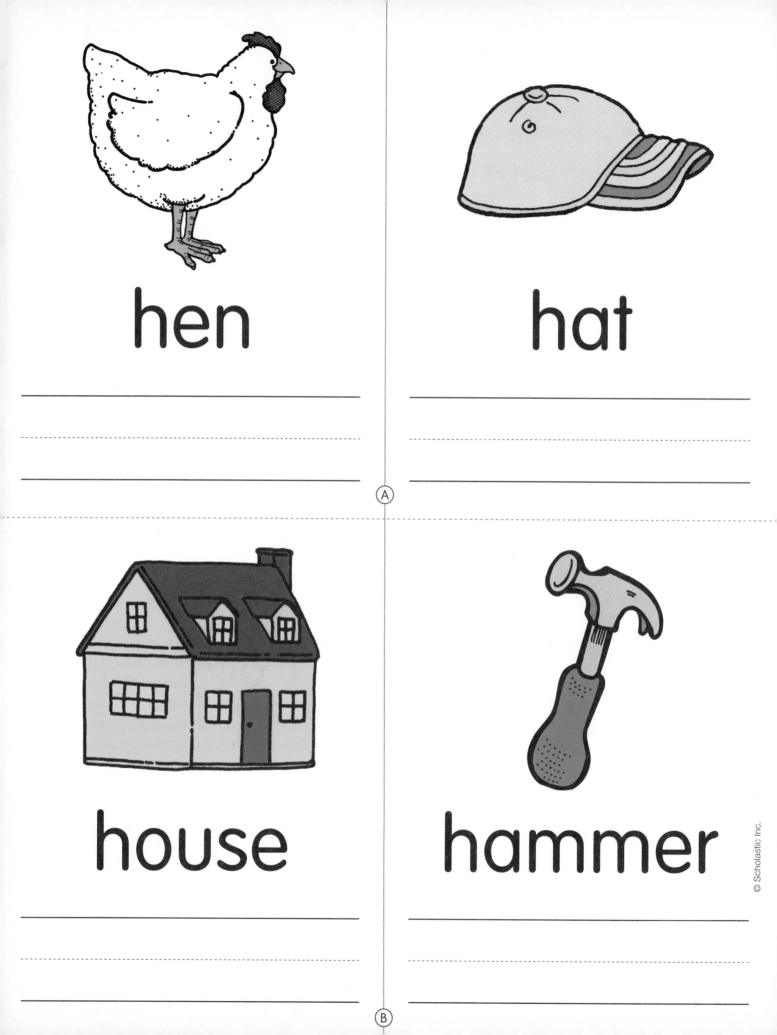

hen

hat

house

hammer

iguana

_____

- - - - - - - - - - -

_____

Ii

insect

_____

- - - - - - - - - - -

_____

ice cream

_____

- - - - - - - - - - -

_____

igloo

iron

ink

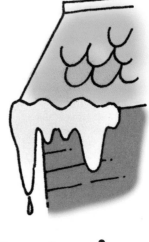

icicle

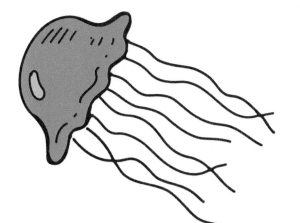

jellyfish

Jj

jacket

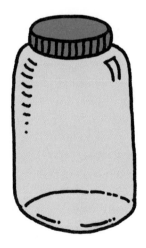

jar

jeans

_____

· · · · · · · · · · · · · ·

_____

jet

_____

· · · · · · · · · · · · · ·

_____

Ⓐ

jump

_____

· · · · · · · · · · · · · ·

_____

JUICE

juice

_____

· · · · · · · · · · · · · ·

_____

Ⓑ

kangaroo

_____

- -

_____

Kk

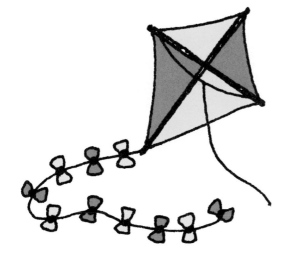

kite

_____

- -

_____

key

_____

- -

_____

kick

king

(A)

kettle

koala

(B)

ladybug

lion

lollipop

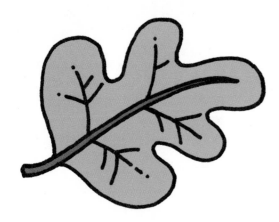

leaf

lamp

Ⓐ

lamb

lemon

Ⓑ

mouse

Alphabet Book

Mm

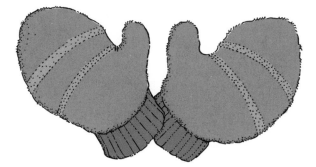

mittens

mask

mouth

mop

milk

moon

newt

_____

- - - - - - - - - - -

_____

Alphabet Book

Nn

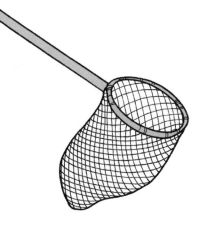

net

_____

- - - - - - - - - - -

nose

_____

- - - - - - - - - - -

nest

nut

newspaper

nail

otter

_____

_____

_____

olive

_____

_____

_____

ostrich

_____

_____

_____

orange

owl

octopus

oval

poodle

_____

- - - - - - - - - - - -

_____

Pp

© Scholastic Inc.

pie

_____

- - - - - - - - - - - -

_____

pig

_____

- - - - - - - - - - - -

_____

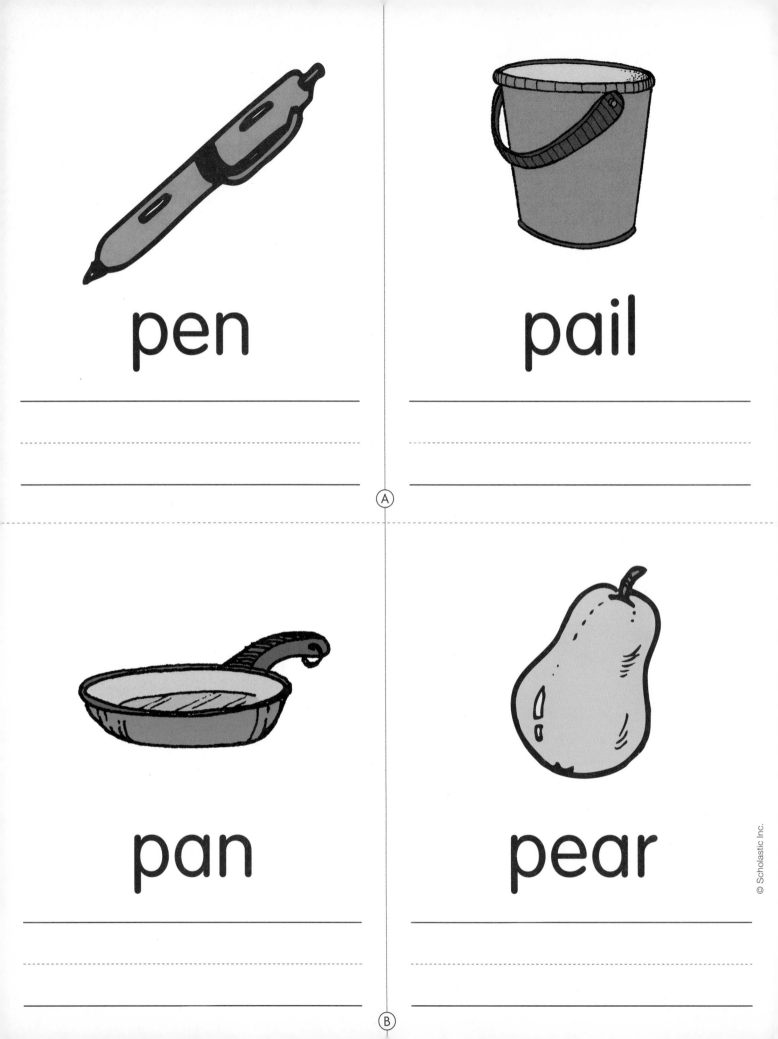

pen

pail

(A)

pan

pear

(B)

quail

_____

- - - - - - - - - - - -

_____

Alphabet Book

Qq

quilt

_____

- - - - - - - - - - - -

queen

_____

- - - - - - - - - - - -

quarter

question

quart

quiet

Ⓐ

Ⓑ

© Scholastic Inc.

rose

R r

rain

rainbow

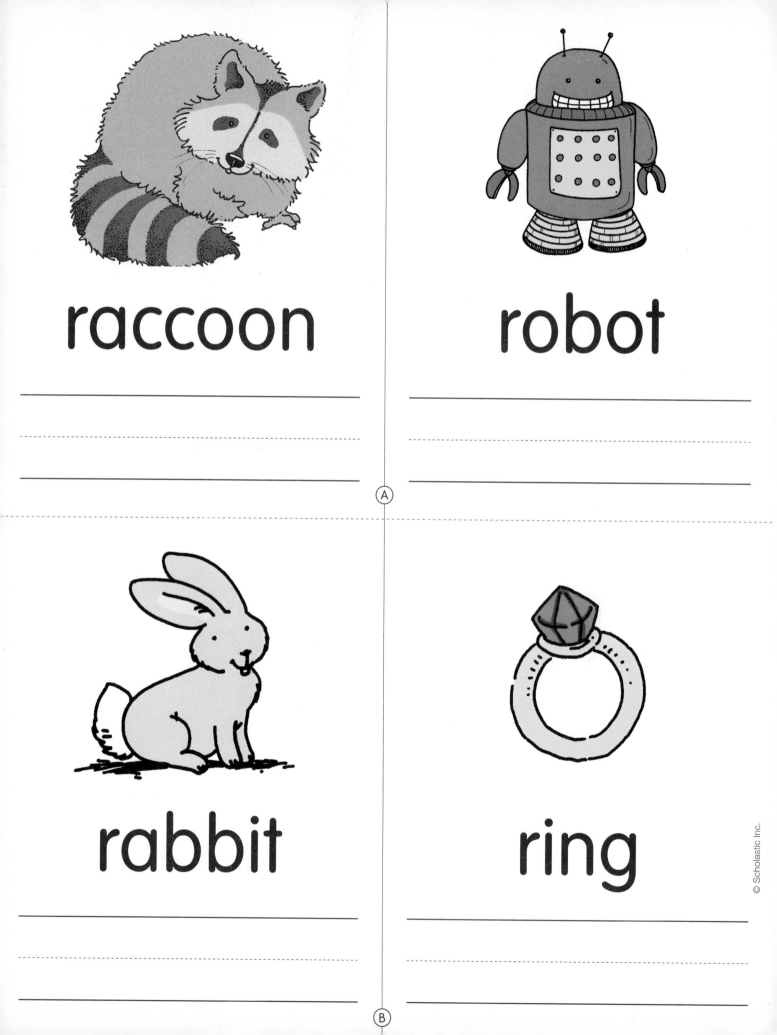

raccoon

robot

rabbit

ring

sun

seahorse

socks

sailboat

_____

seal

_____

(A)

saw

_____

seven

_____

(B)

turtle

Alphabet Book

T t

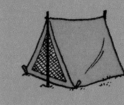 

tent

tiger

toes

tooth

_____

- - - - - - - - - - - - - - - -

_____

Ⓐ

tire

top

_____

- - - - - - - - - - - - - - - -

_____

© Scholastic Inc.

Ⓑ

unicorn

U u

umbrella

underwear

up

unhappy

(A)

unicycle

uniform

(B)

vulture

Alphabet Book

Vv

van

vest

violin

vacuum

Ⓐ

volcano

valentine

Ⓑ

© Scholastic Inc.

walrus

Ww

window

watch

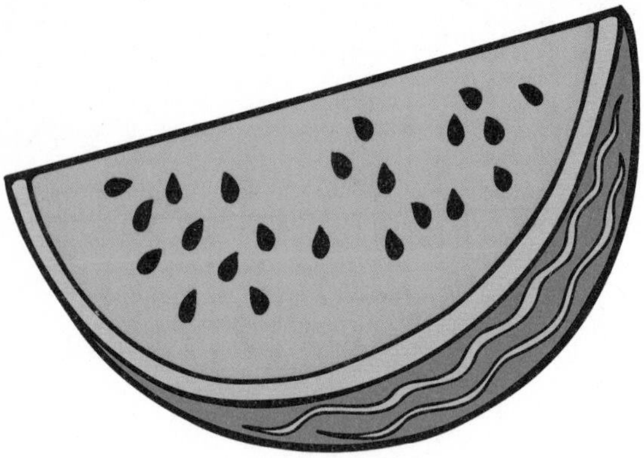

watermelon

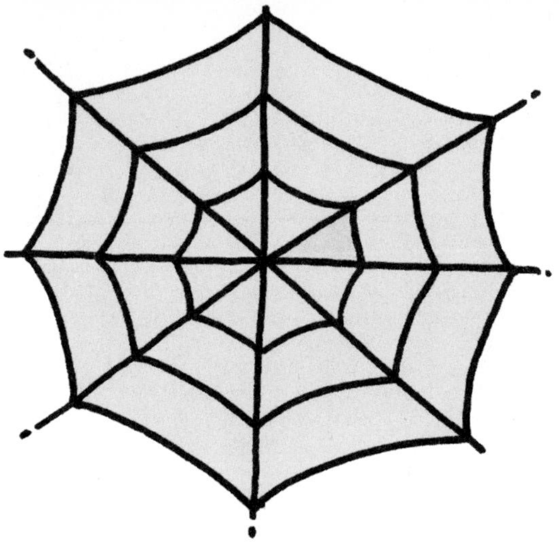

web

worm

wagon

Ⓐ

Ⓑ

x-ray fish

Alphabet Book

X x

x-ray

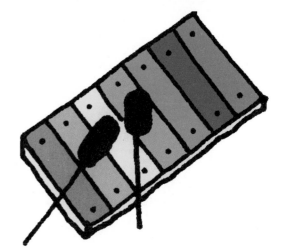

xylophone

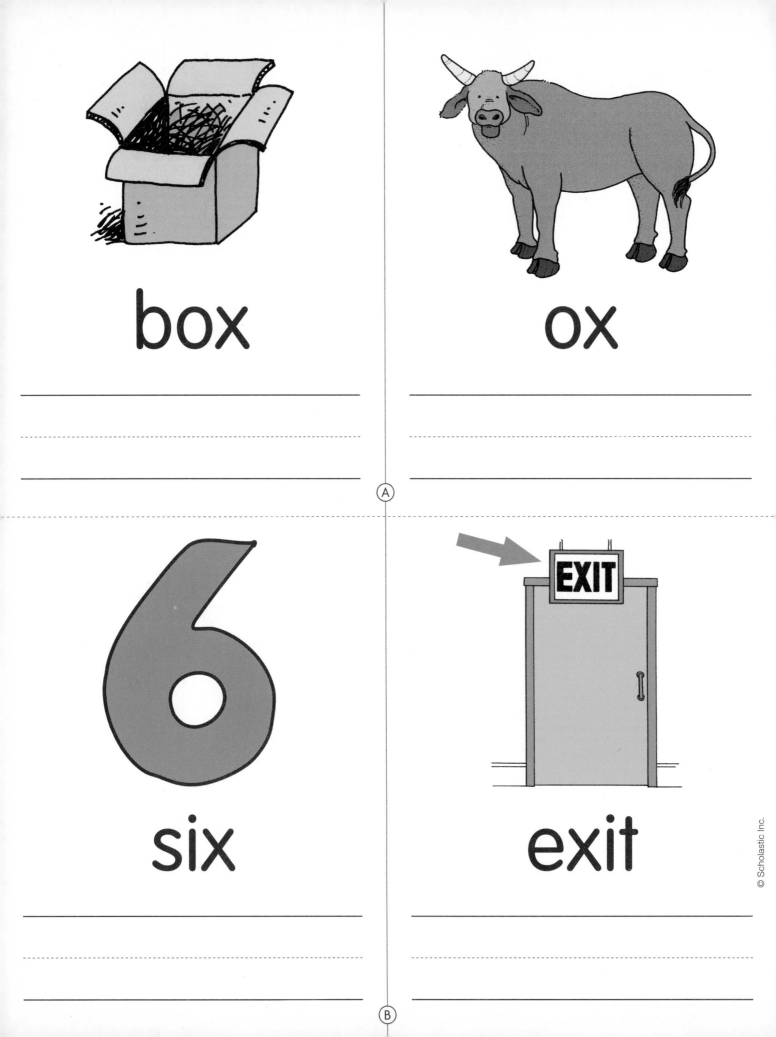

box

ox

six

exit

yak

Alphabet Book

Yy

yo-yo

yarn

yell

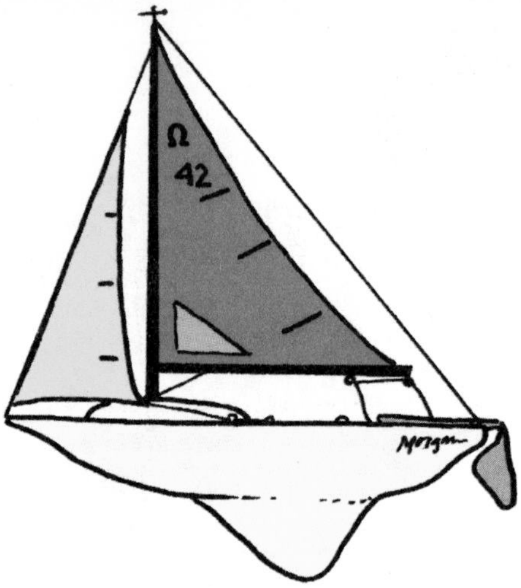

yacht

Ⓐ

yogurt

yawn

Ⓑ

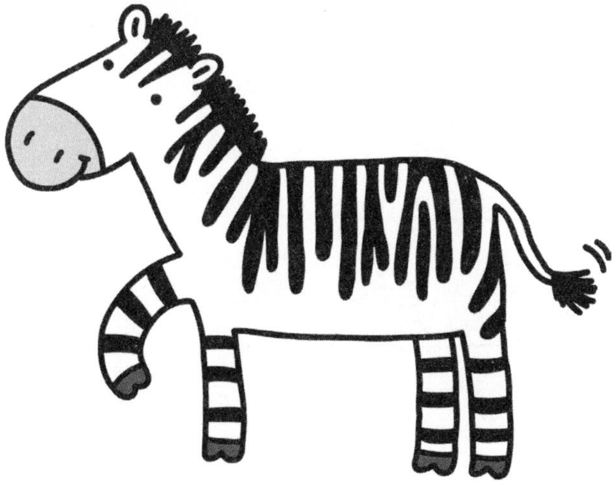

zebra

MY FIRST

Alphabet Book

Zz

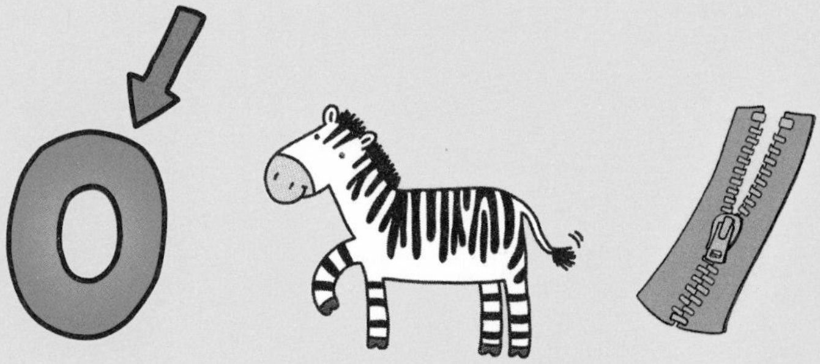

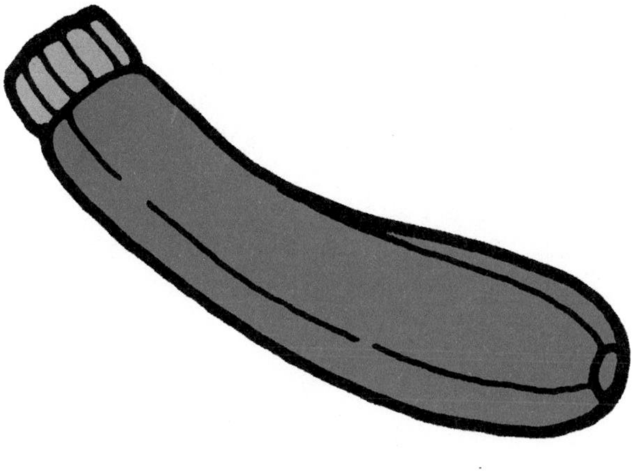

zucchini

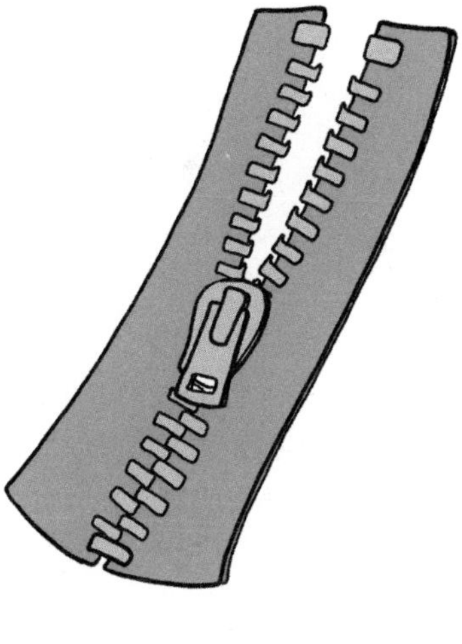

zipper

zigzag

zero

zoo

zeppelin

STK5605687   PO# 550500